PERGAMON INSTITUTE OF ENGLISH (OXFORD)

Language Teaching Methodology Series

Communicative Syllabus Design and Methodology

Other titles in this series include:

See also SYSTEM: *the International Journal of Educational Technology and Language Learning Systems* (sample copy available on request)

Communicative Syllabus Design and Methodology

KEITH JOHNSON

*Centre for Applied Language Studies,
University of Reading, England*

PERGAMON PRESS

Oxford · New York · Toronto · Sydney · Paris · Frankfurt

U.K.	Pergamon Press Ltd., Headington Hill Hall, Oxford OX3 0BW, England
U.S.A.	Pergamon Press Inc., Maxwell House, Fairview Park, Elmsford, New York 10523, U.S.A.
CANADA	Pergamon Press Canada Ltd., Suite 104, 150 Consumers Road, Willowdale, Ontario M2J 1P9, Canada
AUSTRALIA	Pergamon Press (Aust.) Pty. Ltd., P.O. Box 544, Potts Point, N.S.W. 2011, Australia
FRANCE	Pergamon Press SARL, 24 rue des Ecoles, 75240 Paris, Cedex 05, France
FEDERAL REPUBLIC OF GERMANY	Pergamon Press GmbH, Hammerweg 6, D-6242 Kronberg-Taunus, Federal Republic of Germany

First edition 1982

Reprinted 1983

British Library Cataloguing in Publication Data

Johnson, Keith
Communicative Syllabus Design and Methodology—
(Language teaching methodology series)
1. Language and languages—Study and teaching
I. Title   II. Series
407   LB1044.7

ISBN 0-08-025355-5

Library of Congress Catalog Card No: 81-82305

Printed in Great Britain by A. Wheaton & Co. Ltd., Exeter

For

my parents and for Tanya

Acknowledgements

The author and publisher are grateful to the following for permission to reproduce previously published material:

The British Council, *ELT Documents* (Paper 5)
Canadian Modern Language Review (Paper 7)
Oxford University Press, *The Communicative Approach to Language Teaching*, Brumfit and Johnson, 1981 (Papers 10, 13)
Modern English Publications (Papers 8, 14, 16, 17)
Mextesol Journal (Paper 18)
Longman English Teaching Services (Paper 19)

Contents

SECTION 4: METHODOLOGY   145

Introduction

THIS book is a collection of papers, all written between 1976 and 1980, and all concerned with the approach to language teaching which has come to be called "communicative". Some of the papers are published here for the first time, while others have appeared before though sometimes in rather inaccessible journals. The justification for the collection is not that it provides an all-embracing view of the field, taking into account all the valuable work done in the last few years, but it does present one (hopefully coherent) standpoint, and traces its development over a period of time. The reader will be able to discern a movement away from the somewhat "evangelistic" tone of the early papers, through the expression of doubts in the notional/functional syllabus, towards the search for a new type of "communicative" syllabus. The book also reflects a shift of interest away from syllabus design towards methodology. Thus although the papers present one standpoint, it is one that changes and foresees change. Indeed, some of the papers (particularly those looking towards the future) are deliberately speculative in tone. They also cover a wide range from theory to practice. Some (those in Section 3 for example) deal with theoretical issues, while others tackle specific practical problems concerned with materials production and classroom teaching.

There are four sections. The first provides the background and rationale for a communicative approach. It then sketches the Council of Europe team's framework and introduces the concept of the notional/functional syllabus. This section, which has not appeared elsewhere, is intended for the uninitiated and is simpler in style than the rest of the book. Its three papers were written as (and are intended to be read as) a continuous text.

Those already familiar with the Council of Europe's framework and its background should pass directly to Section 2. This deals firstly with practical questions associated with the development of notional/functional syllabuses—as, for example, how one tackles the problem of unit ordering. Then, in Papers 7–9 (and to some extent 6 also), possible areas of application for this type of syllabus are considered. Is it, for example, suitable for use with beginners, with remedial students, and so on?

Section 3 is the most theoretical section. It attempts to confront some of the serious criticisms of a notional/functional approach—many of them already noted in earlier papers. In the light of such criticisms it considers whether new types of syllabus should be sought, and if so what types of syllabus these might be.

Section 4 looks at methodology. The first and last papers (13 and 19) are theoretical, while the others are highly practical. Many of these consider specific exercise types or sequences, and discuss ways in which they may be said to be "communicative". On more than one occasion the papers touch on the implications for syllabus design of the type of methodology being developed. This provides a link between Section 4 and the previous sections.

The book concludes with a short annotated bibliography and a reference list. The bibliography is intended to guide the interested reader through the jungle of literature to those articles and books which he or she will find most useful for further reading.

Keith Johnson   Reading

Section 1:

BACKGROUND

(This section is intended as a general introduction for the "uninitiated" reader.)

Introduction

THE TWENTIETH century has seen the rise—and the fall—of many approaches to language teaching. Anyone who has taught in the field over the past forty years—no matter where in the world he lives—is likely to be painfully aware of this fact. Perhaps he will have begun his career in the certainty (fostered by the pronouncements of his theoretical colleagues, the linguist and the applied linguist) that the task of learning a language involves understanding a large number of sometimes highly complex grammatical rules, together with the development of an ability to translate into and from the foreign language. At some point—earlier or later according to his country's receptiveness to new ideas—his peace will have been shattered by further pronouncements from those same theoretical colleagues who had once provided his security. Successful language learning, he is now told, does not involve intellectual understanding of grammatical rules at all, but is largely a question of habit formation. Translation classes should be replaced by sessions where grammatical structures are drilled until their correct use becomes habit. A struggle with the biology master follows, for the allocation of school funds to purchase that now vital piece of equipment: the language laboratory. No sooner is the battle won, the funds allocated and the laboratory installed, than news begins to filter through of a new dogma: theories concerning the efficacy of drills are, the dogma says, based on a fallacy about language and how it is learned. If we wish to teach a language successfully we must (the message runs) approach the task in a different way. As the biology master suspected all along, the language laboratory turns out to be not such a vital piece of equipment after all.

It is little wonder if over the years the language teacher has developed a healthy scepticism (or even immunity) towards these vagaries of language teaching fashion. Little wonder again if this scepticism is brought to bear on the latest set of ideas which is currently receiving widespread attention, especially when it becomes clear that acceptance of these ideas may imply far-reaching and costly changes in syllabus design, materials production and teacher training programmes. It is appropriate to speak of a "set of ideas" because these have not yet gained the status of a fully-fledged method, nor even of a coherent and unified approach. But they *have* reached that stage in the process of acceptance where they have attracted their own jargon. Suddenly expressions like "communicative language teaching", "notional/functional syllabuses", "needs analysis" are on everyone's lips. The aim of this section is to provide the background essential to understanding what terms like these mean.

There are three papers. The first looks at historical background and attempts to show how a realisation of the need to teach "language use" came about. The second considers some arguments for and against teaching "language use". In the third, the Council of Europe's framework is described and the terms "notional" and "functional" explained. The question of needs analysis is also explored in some detail.

The section discusses these issues in simple terms, and is really intended for the uninitiated reader. Those already initiated may wish to pass directly to Section 2.

Paper 1:

Past and Present Views of Language and Language Teaching

Language Teaching in the Recent Past

MANY approaches to language teaching begin life as reactions to old approaches. Their starting point is often a belief in how languages should *not* be taught, in how the old approaches have failed. Only after a while do the new approaches gain a more positive existence, as they begin to develop their own ideas as to what the task of language teaching involves. One way in which we might begin to consider "communicative language teaching" (the label which characterises the "set of ideas" mentioned in the Introduction above) is therefore to ask "what is it a reaction against?" What characteristic of language teaching in the recent past has led applied linguists to that state of discontent which has made them look for something new?

A Classroom Scene

The scene is a language-teaching classroom somewhere in Britain. The students have been learning English for about four months and today, for the first time, they are meeting the "shall" and "will" forms. They have already come across some modal verbs, like "can" and "must", and the teacher hopes they will remember that these forms, like "shall/will", differ from ordinary verbs in a number of ways. They do not, for example, take an "s" in the third person singular of the simple present tense—we cannot say *"He wills." any more than we can say *"He cans." Again

5

unlike ordinary verbs in English, they do not form the interrogative and negative with part of the verb "do"—*"Does he will?" and *"He doesn't can." are wrong. The students have already learned the contracted forms "can't" and "mustn't", and the short answer forms, "Yes, he can/must", "No, he can't/mustn't." This, the teacher hopes, will help them considerably in learning the contracted and short form answers of "shall/will".

The teacher begins the lesson by introducing "shall" and "will" in a series of "illustrative sentences" given in the coursebook.[1] These sentences show that "shall" is used with "I" and "we", "will" with the other persons. They also illustrate that "shall/will" are associated with the notion of future time. The first set of illustrative sentences are:

> I'm twenty now
> I shall be twenty-one next birthday
> Martin's twenty-two
> He will be twenty-three next birthday

Once the students have assimilated these sentences, the interrogative forms are introduced, and the students immediately begin to practise using substitution tables like this:

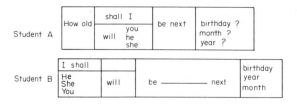

After one or two exercises of this type the negative forms "shan't" and "won't" are introduced, again in illustrative sentences. Practice in these forms is given, and the students read a long passage called "Looking into the Future". It is full of "shalls" and "wills" and here for the first time the students come across the contracted forms "I'll", "he'll", and so on. The lesson is now more than half over, and for the last fifteen minutes the students practise short answers ("Yes, I shall", "No, I shan't", etc.), and all the other "shall/will" forms they have met during the course of the lesson.

After the lesson there is a coffee break, and when this is over the students go to the language laboratory. Here they are given a number of drills using "shall" and "will". In one drill a voice on the tape says things like:

Will he come? Will he dance?
Will they work tomorrow? Will they work on Sunday?
Will Bill ask her? Will she say yes?
Will you play the violin? Will I like it?

Each time the student must respond with a sentence like "He'll come, but he won't dance", "They'll work tomorrow, but they won't work on Sunday."

By the end of this session the students have been given extremely extensive practice in the various forms of "shall" and "will". As they are leaving the laboratory one of the students, who has been learning English slightly longer than the others, comes to the teacher with a problem. He has heard people in England using "going to" to indicate future time— in sentences like "I'm going to stay at home tomorrow."— and he wants to know if there is any difference between "going to" and "shall/will". It is a good question, and the teacher knows that at some stage she will have to explain the relationship between the various forms in English used to indicate future time reference—including "going to" and the simple present tense. But "going to" has not yet been introduced in the coursebook the class is using, and the teacher would rather wait until it is before giving an explanation.

The teacher is quite content with the way the two lessons have gone. All the students are now able to produce the various forms of "shall" and "will" with comparative ease, and they seem to understand what the forms "mean" or "signify". They have grasped, that is, the association between "shall/will" and future time, and although there are still many problems of "signification" to be met—and distinguishing between "going to" and "shall/will" is one of them—things are at least so far clear. The teacher is also well pleased with the coursebook she is using. The "shall/will" unit is the penultimate unit in the first coursebook of the series, and the teacher has already decided to use Book 2 with her students. The course is well graded. It follows a sequence which introduces the students to the grammar of the language in easily assimilated stages. For example, the first twelve units of the book cover the following structures:

1. This/that is a *noun*. It's a/the *noun*.

2. This is *possessive + noun*. These are (no article) *plural noun*.

3. The *noun* is *adjective*. *Pronoun* is an *adjective + noun*.

4. *Subject* is *adverbial phrase*. *Subject* is *place adverb*.

5. There is a *noun + place adverb*. How many *plural noun* are there?

6. *Noun* is as *adjective* as *noun*. *Noun* is made of *substance*.

7. There is some *unaccountable noun*. There are some *plural noun*. *Subject* has *object*.

8. Are there any *plural noun?* Is there any *uncountable noun?*

9. *Subject* is *-ing + adverbial phrase*.

10. Subject is *-ing + object*.

11. *Imperative + name.   Imperative + (direct   object) + (adverbial phrase)*.

12. *Verb + object pronoun. Preposition + object pronoun. Subject + verb + indirect object + direct object*.

The Emphasis on Mastery of Language Structure

Teachers of English as a Foreign Language will recognise these lessons as being fairly typical of many given almost everywhere in the world in recent years. They illustrate one of the characteristic features of language teaching since about the fifties—the emphasis placed on what Newmark and Reibel (1968) call "mastery of language structure". Both the teacher giving the lesson and the materials producer recognise that if the students are to become proficient in the language, they must master the *mechanisms* by which the language works. They must learn the *language system*. These two lessons concentrated on one small, but nevertheless fairly complex part of the English language system—the verbs "shall" and "will". Every activity the students are asked to do is geared to this sole aim of familiarising them with the mechanisms by which this part of the system works—how positives, negatives, inter-rogatives, contracted forms, short answer forms are made. And in both classroom and laboratory sessions the students are given plenty of practice in manipulating these structures, until their use becomes almost automatic.

This emphasis on language structure is also reflected in the choice of language to which the students are exposed in these lessons. The "Looking into the Future" passage is an example of this. It is clear why this passage is included in the unit. It is not intended to stand as an example of authentic modern English prose. It has been specially concocted for the occasion, to contain as many "shalls" and "wills" per paragraph as possible, illustrated in a large variety of sentence types.

The way in which the coursebook as a whole is organised also clearly shows how much importance is placed on language structure. Part of the book's syllabus—for the first twelve units—has been illustrated above. It is a list of structures, grouped and graded in such a way as to facilitate learning as much as possible. Each unit—like the unit we described being taught—deals with a small number of (usually related) structures, and the course as a whole aims to cover the main structures of the English language system. All teachers of English are familiar with this type of syllabus; indeed, if we were to compare this syllabus with others used throughout the world, we would be struck by how similar they are. Structural syllabuses have over the years come to look remarkably alike.[2]

The lessons which we witnessed earlier do not concentrate *exclusively* on language structure. The teacher did pay some attention to signifi-cation—making it clear to the students that "shall" and "will" signify futurity—and she is well aware that further explanation (in particular of the relationship between "shall/will" and the various other forms used in English to signify futurity) will be necessary. But the emphasis is heavily on language structure, not only in these lessons, but in much recent language teaching.

A word which captures this characteristic is the word "systemic".[3] An approach which emphasises teaching the language *system* is a systemic approach. Its primary aim is to teach the students to handle the language system competently, to teach what might be called "systemic compet-ence". It is a perfectly reasonable aim and common sense, if nothing else, tells us that no-one can communicate successfully in a foreign language unless they have this systemic competence. Indeed, language teaching has never at any point in its history been able to ignore the teaching of structures, and the only thing which characterises the recent past is the degree of emphasis that has been placed on this aim.

If this aim is so reasonable, then what has "communicative language teaching" found deficient in this systemic approach? Why are we now seeking a different approach to teaching languages, and what is this new approach? To answer these questions adequately, it is necessary to turn for a moment to the realm of linguistic theory.

The Linguistic Background

The Emphasis on Language Structure

There is a particular historical reason why a systemic approach to language teaching has been so pronounced over the past few decades. It is that linguistics itself has carried the same emphasis over the same period.[4] Language teachers have always looked to the linguist for guidance on how to teach languages. It is natural for the language teacher to regard linguistics as something of a mother discipline; after all, he is concerned with "teaching something which is the object of study of linguistics, and is described by linguistic methods" (Halliday, McIntosh and Strevens, 1964, p. 166). It is small wonder, then, that trends in linguistics should be reflected in the language teaching classroom.

"Many linguists nowadays", Christophersen (1973, p. 13) observes, "regard the analysis of linguistic structure as their central and perhaps their only concern." It was certainly their central concern during and before the early fifties when the post-Bloomfieldian school of linguistics was flourishing. The goal of what has come to be known as "structural linguistics" was simply to develop a system of identifying and classifying the structures occurring in a given language. Little or no consideration was given to how the structures might be used, and as long as they were classified according to rigorously "scientific" criteria, the linguist was happy. 1957 saw the publication of Chomsky's *Syntactic Structures*. This book heralded the arrival of transformational generative grammar (TGG), the school of linguistics which has remained more or less predominant ever since. The goals of TGG are different from those of structural linguistics, yet the emphasis on language structure remains. One area in which we may see this characteristic clearly present is the study of child language acquisition—the study, that is, of how the young child acquires its mother tongue. For a variety of reasons, language acquisition studies gained a new lease of life with the advent of Chomsky's theories, and since 1957 many books and papers have been written on the subject. Sometimes these studies consider one small area of the language's syntax, and trace the child's progress towards mastery of it. An example of this type of study is Bellugi (1967). She is concerned with the way a group of children come to acquire the English negation system—how they progress from simple two-word negative utterances like "no heavy", through sentence negation using an initial "no" (as in "No the sun shining.") to eventual mastery of negation using auxiliaries ("The sun isn't shining."). Other studies such as Brown and Fraser (1964), Menyuk (1969) and many more, consider large areas of syntax and attempt to find regularities and general principles in the child's acquisition of them. Both these kinds of studies have one element in common. They are concerned with how the child learns to master the structures of the language—the language system. How, in other words, it comes to acquire "systemic competence".

This, then, is the linguistic climate in which the systemic approach to language teaching developed and flourished. It is one in which the predominant interest lay in studying the language system. But recently the climate has begun to change, and it is this change that provides the linguistic background to communicative language teaching. One of the areas in which the systemic approach to linguistics was first challenged was in fact that of child language acquisition. In an article appearing in 1970, Campbell and Wales argue that if we wish to understand language acquisition, then studies of how the child learns the grammatical and phonological systems—studies such as those mentioned above—are not enough. We have to consider not only how the child acquires *systemic competence*, but also aspects of a more general question, namely how it learns to *communicate*. Or, to use the term Campbell and Wales adopt, how it develops *communicative competence*.

Communicative, and Systemic, Competence

What is communicative competence? Clearly it is something which involves systemic competence—the ability to form grammatically correct sentences. The student (or child) who fails to master the syntactic rules governing the use of "shall" and "will"—who produces abominations like *"Does he will?", *"He wills." or *"He will going."—will certainly at the very least obscure the message he wishes to communicate. Indeed, most teachers of English as a Foreign Language can think of many examples of situations in which students' grammatical mistakes not merely obscure the message but result in the wrong message being conveyed—as for example when the foreign doctor confuses "must have" and "had to" and tells his patient "I'm afraid I must have amputated your leg." Systemic competence is a part (and a very important part) of communicative competence, whether we are talking about the student learning a foreign language or the child learning its first language.

But there is more to the business of communicating than the ability to produce grammatically correct utterances, as we can clarify by means of a hypothetical example. Imagine that we could build a computer which has perfect mastery of English grammar, phonology and lexis. This computer (let us call it the "Syntactically Perfect Electronically Activated Computer—SPEAK for short) has, in other words, absolute systemic competence. SPEAK can produce sentences using "shall" and "will"—like "You will come tomorrow.", for example—without difficulty. Like the students in the lessons we witnessed earlier, SPEAK knows that "will" rather than "shall" should be used when the subject pronoun is "you"; it knows that "will" should be correctly followed by an infinitive without "to". SPEAK also has perfect knowledge of the rules of signification, and it knows (as the students would grasp during their lessons on "shall/will") that these forms can signifiy futurity. Had SPEAK produced *"You will come yesterday.", we would be justified in doubting its knowledge of signification.

SPEAK, then, always gets its grammar right, and always observes the rules of signification. In fact, this computer is a kind of idealisation of the student who follows an entire language course of the type we looked at earlier. But is this systemic knowledge enough to ensure that SPEAK will be able to communicate adequately? Most certainly not, for apart from being able to form grammatically correct sentences, SPEAK must also know *when* to use them. Consider one possible use of the sentence "You will come tomorrow." It might be used as a strong command given by an angry father to his disobedient son. In this sense it might even have the overtone of a threat—something along the lines of "You'd better make sure you come, or else. . . ." But it would not be used where a modicum of politeness is required, as for example when a manager is telling (politely, but nevertheless as an order) his subordinate to attend a meeting tomorrow, in which case "Please come tomorrow." or "I'd like you to come tomorrow." would be appropriate. SPEAK's knowledge of grammar and signification would give it no information that as a command "You will come tomorrow." is appropriate in one situation, but not the other. And if SPEAK does not know when to use this sentence (as well as, equally importantly, when *not* to use it), he will soon earn the reputation of a grammatically correct but exceedingly bad-mannered computer—one which, for all its systemic knowledge, does not know how to give a polite order.

SPEAK's knowledge lets it down in a number of ways, and one of the most important is that it does not provide the computer with a "sense of appropriateness", the knowledge of how to say the right thing at the right time. In a sense the major criticism that Campbell and Wales level at the systemic approach to child language acquisition is just that it treats the child like a "systemic computer", failing to consider how the child builds up "the ability to produce or understand utterances which are not so much *grammatical* but, more importantly, *appropriate to the context in which they are made*" (1970, p. 247—the italics are in the original). If we try to study the utterances made by children without considering the linguistic and non-linguistic contexts in which they are made, we cannot possibly gain any insight into how the child develops this essential skill of correctly linking utterance to context. Campbell and Wales suggest ways in which we may study child language with a view to discovering how communicative, rather than just systemic, competence is developed.

The theme of appropriateness is also taken up by Hymes in an article entitled "On Communicative Competence" (1970). Linguists—particularly of the transformational school—have, he argues, been concerned almost exclusively with what he calls "the possible". They have focused their attention on what the rules of the language system permit as possible structures. But, he claims, if we confine our study to a consideration of "the possible", we shall learn little about how language is used as a means of communication between humans. Of the various other factors which need to be taken into account, one of the most important is that of appropriateness. But there are others, including what Hymes calls "feasibility". This is another aspect of language use which SPEAK's knowledge (the knowledge of the "possible") would give it no insight into. The sequence "The mouse the cat the dog the man the woman married beat chased ate had a white tail." is a possible sentence. It is perfectly grammatical, being merely an extension of the more easily understood "The mouse the cat ate had a white tail." But it would never be used by a normal native speaker (linguists not being counted in this category!) in normal communicative situations. It is systemically possible, but not feasible, and if SPEAK's knowledge is confined to the systemic we might expect it to produce sentences like this.

The articles by Campbell and Wales and Hymes exemplify a shift which is at present taking place within linguistics. It is a shift *away from* the study of language seen purely as a system; away from the study of "the possible". It is a shift *towards* the study of language as communication; towards the study of (among other factors) "the appropriate". Since this shift in emphasis provides the theoretical background to communicative language teaching, it is worthwhile taking time to consider some work being done in this "new" tradition.[5] In this way we may hope to gain some insight into the rationale behind present attempts to make language teaching "communicative".

Examples of the "New" Linguistic Approach

i) *Halliday*

For a number of years Halliday has been exploring ways of classifying the linguistic means by which we may carry out certain functions or tasks. For example, in Halliday (1973) he considers how we might perform the function of "scolding a naughty child". He imagines a situation in which a small child has been playing on a building site, and comes home holding some object which he found there. The boy's mother disapproves; she wishes to express her disapproval and prevent him from doing the same thing again. There are a number of things she might say. Here are seven:[6]

1. You're very naughty.
2. I'll smack you if you do that again.
3. I don't like you to do that.
4. That thing doesn't belong to you.
5. Daddy would be very cross.
6. You make Mummy very unhappy by disobeying.
7. That's not allowed.

There are various ways in which these sentences might be classified. One is in terms of the type of control used. For example, in (1) the mother is attempting to control the child's behaviour by expressing disapproval, and in (2) she uses a threat. (3) has more the quality of an appeal, while in (4) she is attempting to indicate to the child that his behaviour breaks the "rules of society". Here is a slightly modified version of Halliday's classification (1973, p. 74). The numbers in brackets refer to the sentences above.

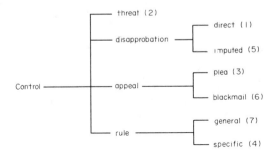

This is only the beginning of Halliday's analysis. He continues by trying to discover linguistic characteristics associated with each type of control. He notes, for example, that a threat is (to use his specialised linguistic terminology) "likely to be realised as a transitive clause of action with "you" as Goal, and with a verb of a particular sub-class as Process, in simple future tense". Then he considers other possible means of classification. Instead of analysing the seven sentences in terms of control we may, for example, consider what Halliday calls their orientation. In sentence (4) reference is made to the object the child has taken; the sentence is "orientated" towards the object. In the other sentences the orientation is a person—the child in (1), the father in (5) and the mother in (6). The orientation of each sentence affects its linguistic form in ways Halliday explores. The result of his complex analysis is what he calls a "semantic network" which classifies the means of 'scolding a child" and specifies linguistic characteristics of each classification.

The details of Halliday's analysis are not relevant here. What is important to notice is how different it is from the kind of analysis we have come to expect from linguists working within recently predominant traditions. Linguists normally analyse utterances to discover what they reveal about the workings of the language system. For example, let a transformational linguist loose on these seven sentences and one of the facts he might note is that the first—"You're very naughty."—has the structure:

$$\frac{pronoun + \text{"be"} + modifying\ adverb + adjective}{\text{You} + \text{'re} + \text{very} + \text{naughty}}$$

In this way it is superficially similar to sentences like "You're very young." and "You're very late." But, he would point out, while "You're very naughty." has the related form "That's very naughty of you.", the other two sentences do not have similarly related forms. In English we cannot say *"that's very young of you." or *"That's very late of you." The transformational linguist would then try to discover why this should be. The purpose of his exercise would be to find out something about the way English works as a system. He has little interest in discovering how or when the sentences are used, and is concerned only with whether or not they are *possible*, and why. Halliday, on the other hand, takes the use to which the sentences are being put as his starting point. The sentences he selects for analysis are chosen not because they provide interesting examples of English grammatical structures, but because they may have one common function. His initial question is not "how does the English grammatical system operate?", but rather, "how do we use English to perform one chosen function: that of scolding a child".

Later in this paper we shall consider the implications of this type of approach for language teaching. At that point it will be important to realise just how central Halliday's initial question type is to his view of language and linguistics. According to this view, "the internal organisation of language is not arbitrary but embodies a positive reflection of the functions that language has evolved to serve in the life of social man" (Halliday, 1970a). We can, in other words, only really understand language as a system if we study it in relation to how it is used.

If we apply this view to language acquisition we would reach the conclusion that approaches (like the transformational studies mentioned above) which examine how structures are acquired without reference to how those structures are used, are not merely missing out a "dimension". Much more fundamentally, they cannot really hope to understand the process of language acquisition. It is not that these studies are incomplete so much as that they are based on shaky foundations.

ii) *Sinclair and Coulthard*

The work of Sinclair and Coulthard (1975) will be taken as a second example of the shift in emphasis currently taking place in linguistics. They set themselves the task of analysing interactions between teachers and pupils in the school classroom. Not surprisingly, at various points in their investigation they come across situations in which teacher and pupils misunderstand each other. In one lesson, for example, the teacher plays a recording of a television programme "in which there is a psychologist talking with a 'posh' accent. The teacher wants to explore the children's attitude to accent and the value judgements based on it" (p. 29). When the recording is finished the teacher questions the students about the psychologist. The teacher says:

> Teacher: What kind of a person do you think he is?
> Do you—(pupil bursts out laughing) what are you laughing at?
> Pupil: Nothing.

The pupil says "Nothing" because she thinks the teacher is angry with her for laughing. She interprets the teacher's interrogative "What are you laughing at?" as an implied command to stop laughing. In fact the teacher does not mean it in this way. He intends it as a serious question; if he can make the pupil explain why she is laughing, this will provide him with an excellent opening for the topic he wishes to discuss. As the conversation proceeds, the pupil realises what the teacher really meant and the misunderstanding is cleared up.

It is easy to see why misunderstanding should have taken place. Some interrogatives in English—such as "What are you laughing at?", "Why are you shouting?", "What are you standing up for?"—may be interpreted either as straight requests for information, or as commands to do something expressed in a rather indirect way. Because sentences like these may have two possible interpretations, the question arises how a pupil (or, in more general terms, any native speaker) knows in any given situation which interpretation is the correct one. In the case we have considered there was misunderstanding; but more often than not the listener will know immediately and unequivocally whether the speaker is asking for information or giving a command. Sometimes the speaker will give a "linguistic signal" to make his meaning clear; for example, his intonation or tone may indicate that he is giving a command. But often there will be no such signal, and only the listener's perception of the situation will guide him to the correct interpretation.

Sinclair and Coulthard try to draw up rules which specify what situational factors have to be present for a declarative or an interrogative to be interpretable as a command. One rule says that "any declarative or interrogative [uttered by a teacher in a classroom] is to be interpreted as a *command to stop* if it refers to an action or activity which is proscribed at the time of the utterance" (p. 32). According to this rule, utterances like:

I can hear someone laughing.

Is someone laughing?

What are you laughing at?

are to be taken as commands to stop laughing in situations where laughing is felt to be a "forbidden activity". Where laughing is *not* a forbidden activity, these three utterances would receive quite different interpretations. The first might simply be an observation, and the second and third requests for information. The pupil's misunderstanding in the episode outlined earlier happens because (contrary to the teacher's intentions) she perceives of laughing as a forbidden activity in that particular classroom situation.

In fact Sinclair and Coulthard give three rules for the interpretation of declaratives or interrogatives as commands. But once again, the details of the analysis are irrelevant here. What is important is to understand the nature of the questions which many linguists are now asking. They are questions of "language use". Sinclair and Coulthard wish to find out what rules determine whether a particular piece of language is to be used as a command or as a request for information. Notice that a structural analysis of the three sentences just considered will not provide this information. It would identify the first sentence as a declarative containing the sequence "$can + infinitive + object + $"$-ing$" form. The second and third sentences would be recognised as interrogatives, the second being a so-called "yes/no" question, and the third a "Wh-" question. The analysis would not concern itself with whether the sentences could be used as commands or as requests for information. It would say something about the sentences' structure, nothing about their uses.

The work of Halliday and Sinclair and Coulthard has been introduced to illustrate the linguistic tradition which has provided the theoretical background to communicative language teaching. They are but two examples of what is in fact a widespread area of study stretching beyond the bounds of linguistics into other disciplines. Candlin (1976) in fact lists ten areas which have contributed to the development of communicative language teaching. They range from the work of philosophers like Austin (1962) and Searle (1969) to that of ethnologists such as Hymes and Labov who have a special interest in language. For more detailed reference to background areas, see Brumfit and Johnson (1979, pp. 24–5).

Communicative Competence and Language Teaching

One way in which these theoretical areas might be relevant to the practical question of teaching languages becomes clear if we ask ourselves a fundamental question—one in fact so fundamental that any language teaching method implicitly provides some answer to it. The question is, what does a person have to "know" in order to have mastered a foreign language properly? Part of the answer is that he certainly has to know how the language operates as a system. He must master the systemic rules of the language, and the rules governing the formation of "shall/will" sentences are examples of these. As can be seen from the lessons we looked at earlier, teachers have not failed to recognise the importance of learning these kinds of rules.

Knowledge of signification is clearly also important. The student who does not know that "shall/will" can be used to signify (among other things) future time reference will be unable to use this part of the language system correctly. Again, teachers have recognised that signification needs to be taught. Whenever a new form is introduced at least one of its significations is given, and teachers often spend considerable time clarifying distinctions in the signification of easily confused forms—such as present perfect and simple past, "since" and "ago", etc.

But there is a third type of knowledge that he must possess— knowledge concerned with language use. As our example of the computer indicated, systemic knowledge and knowledge of signification do not ensure that SPEAK will be able to give an order in a way appropriate to a given situation. It may know how to form grammatical sentences and how to signify future time; but it does not know how to order. The parallel between SPEAK and the students who learned "shall/will" in the lessons described earlier has already been drawn. Both can and cannot do the same things. And in order to satisfy his communicative needs, the student must know the "rules of use".

What are these communicative needs? They are unlikely perhaps to include SPEAK's "giving commands", because many (though not all) students are unlikely to need English for this purpose; and they are even more unlikely to include Halliday's "scolding a child". But there are a host of other things which we can reasonably predict our students will want to do with English—to greet, introduce people, ask for information, apologise, warn, advise, persuade, complain, and many more. Yet how often are students taught how to do these things? The phenomenon of the "systemic student" is all too common. He has learned English for many years in his native country; he knows the grammar well, his pronunciation is good and his vocabulary wide. Yet when he steps off the plane on his first visit to England, he may find difficulty in performing even the most simple communicative tasks, like buying a ticket for the airport bus, or greeting a British friend who meets him at the airport.

We have said that (in extremely general terms) communicative competence involves three types of "knowledge"—of grammar, signification and use. We have further implied that whereas language teaching in the past has considered the first two, it has neglected the third—hence the "systemic student phenomenon". In fact Widdowson (1972) convincingly illustrates how traditional teaching procedures may actually obscure facts about use. He cites the common procedure for teaching the present continuous tense in English. In order to convey that one signification of this tense is to refer to an action at present taking place, the teacher might (for example) walk to the door and say "I'm walking to the door." She might then ask others to do similar actions, while selected students say "Maria is combing her hair", Fritz and Elke are closing the door" and so on. The *use* to which these sentences are here being put is that of giving a commentary: the teacher is commentating on her own actions, and the students on the actions of each other. It is not of course usual to commentate in this way, and we are therefore teaching an unnatural use of language. Equally importantly, the procedure fails to illustrate far more important uses of the tense, as for example in answer to requests for information:

A: Where's John?
B: He's talking to Mike at the moment.
   He's coming in a minute.

Thus by adopting this common procedure we may succeed in teaching *signification*, but we fail to teach use.

According to the type of argument developed over the past few pages, then, past language teaching has neglected the area of use. Our response might therefore be to add a new dimension to the teaching by means of which we compensate for this neglect and deliberately make it our aim to teach use. This might well lead to "two-stage programmes" in which we initially teach structures in relation to signification and then, at a second stage, tackle the teaching of use.

But how convincing is this type of argument? Can we really compartmentalise communicative competence into various types of knowledge and suggest that one type may be taught after the others, in a kind of sequence. According to Halliday's view, discussed on page 17, this would not be the case. For him, language structures cannot be understood as a system without reference to use; perhaps therefore structures should not be *taught* without reference to use. In this case, a "two-stage operation" would be inappropriate; we should from the very start teach structures in relation to their uses.

There are then two possible responses to the "new" linguistic tradition, and at various points in this book the conflict between these responses will be discussed.[7] But one thing seems certain; that somehow or other we need to teach use. Or do we? All that has in fact so far been said is that knowledge of language use is necessary, and this does not automatically mean it need be taught. After all (to choose an extreme example) another skill which the student must possess is the ability to move the vocal chords in a way that produces sound. But this ability does not need to be taught since it is one which the learner brings with him to the task of language learning. Is the same true of the ability to use language appropriately? Some would claim that we need not teach this; others that we cannot, and still others that we should not. Since these claims are fairly widespread, they deserve careful attention and will form the topic of a separate paper.

Notes

1. The coursebook is Broughton (1968). The points made here are not intended in any sense as criticism, and the book has been chosen as one of the more enlightened examples of the tradition being discussed.
2. The similarity of structural syllabuses throughout the world was pointed out to me by L. G. Alexander.
3. The word "systemic" is used by different writers in different senses. It is here being used as an adjective related to the noun "system", and not in the specialised sense of "systemic grammar" used by Halliday and others.
4. The emphasis on the analysis of language structure without regard to meaning is far more characteristic of American than of European linguistics, and this difference has reflected itself in language teaching practice.
5. The word "new" is used, for want of a better label, to distinguish tradition from the one just discussed. In fact, as implied in Note 4, the tradition is by no means new. Indeed, one way of viewing the background to communicative language teaching is not as a reaction against the American tradition at all, but as a natural development from European (especially British) linguistics.
6. For the purposes of explication, Halliday's examples and discussion have been simplified and slightly changed.
7. See particularly Papers 9 and 11.

Teaching Language Use: Some Arguments for and against

The Need to Teach Language Use

THERE are three sorts of commonly heard argument which suggest that the teaching of use is unnecessary. The first claims that once the student has mastered the language system, he has all the information he requires to *use* the language correctly. We have already seen that this is in fact untrue, but the matter is worth exploring a little further. Teachers (and indeed some linguists) often mistakenly equate structure and function (or use). One example would be the identification of the imperative structure with the function of ordering. Statements like "the imperative is used to order" and "orders are expressed by use of the imperative" are misleading if the impression they leave with the students is that all imperatives are orders, and all orders are imperatives. Here are three imperative sentences:[1]

1. Be quiet.
2. Have some coffee.
3. Give us this day our daily bread.

The most likely use of (1) would be as an order. (2) is not an order at all, but an offer, while (3) is neither an order nor offer, but a plea. These sentences are structurally similar, yet their uses are quite different. Structurally similar sentences need not be used in the same way.

It is equally untrue to say that all orders are imperatives. We have already seen one example of an interrogative interpreted as an order— the misunderstood teacher's "What are you laughing at?". In certain circumstances and with certain intonations the following might also be correctly interpreted in the same way:

4. I hope you'll close the window.
5. Would you close the window.
6. It's cold in here.

Despite the fact that these sentences might be used in the same way, they are structurally quite different from each other. (4) and (6) are both declarative in form, but in other structural respects are quite dissimilar. (5) is an interrogative.

Grammatically similar sentences, then, may be used in quite different ways, while sentences being used in a similar way may be grammatically quite dissimilar. It is easy to see how a false equation between structure and use leads to the belief that the latter need not be taught. For if all imperatives were orders, then by teaching our students the imperative we would at the same time automatically be teaching them how to order. But the equation *is* a false one, and this fact suggests the necessity for teaching language use.

A second argument runs along similar lines. It claims that if the student knows what all the words and structures in the language *signify*, teaching language use becomes unnecessary. To examine this claim we might further explore SPEAK's sentence "You will come tomorrow." One possible use of this sentence was mentioned, that of giving an emphatic command. There are of course other possible uses. In a certain context and with a certain stress it might function as a reassurance, something along the lines of "Don't worry, I'll see to it you'll be allowed to come tomorrow." In different circumstances it might have the force of "I can see that whatever I say you have made up your mind to come."— an expression of resignation perhaps. These, then, are three possible uses of the sentence.

So far we have applied the term "signification" to individual structures only. We have for example said that one signification of "shall/will" is to refer to future time, and that the present continuous tense may signify contiguous action. But the concept may of course be used to characterise entire sentences—for example, the computer's "You will come tomorrow." The signification of the constituent parts might be said to be (in extremely rough and grossly oversimplified terms):

You   —the person I am addressing (singular or plural)

will   —future time

come   —present oneself at the place where I am/was/shall be

tomorrow—the day following day

By a process of combination the entire sentence comes to signify something like (assuming a singular male "you"): "The person I am addressing is going to present himself at the place where I shall be at some future time—namely, the day following today."

This analysis of signification tells SPEAK nothing about how the sentence might be used—whether as a command, a reassurance or an expression of resignation. Nor (as pointed out in the previous paper) does it tell the computer that in its command function, the sentence is appropriate in the "angry father to disobedient child" situation, but not in the "manager to subordinate" situation. The uses to which a sentence might be put cannot be ascertained from an analysis of the signification of its constituent parts, and a student who knows what all the words and structures in the language signify, does not necessarily know how to use the language correctly.

Some would put forward a third argument why language use need not be taught. It is based on the belief that the rules of use are the same in every language. The way we greet, invite, request information is, they would claim, the same in French, German or any other language. As long as the student is able to translate on a fairly literal level from native into foreign language, he will be able to communicate adequately. Anyone who has lived for any length of time in a foreign language community will know that, as an increasing amount of sociolinguistic literature attests, that is just not true. The following examples illustrate.

Keenan and Ochs (1979) are concerned with Malagasy, the language of Madagascar. They speak of a situation in which a European enters a village where he is well known and asks some women in the courtyard for one of his friends. After some discussion the wife of the friend appears on the scene and says that the friend isn't there. You say you wonder when he'll return, to which she responds, "Well, if you don't come after dinner you won't catch him."

Keenan and Ochs note that His use of a double negative would be interpreted as unco-operative in Western society. One might think the wife perhaps is being coy, but certainly is not giving as much information as she could. But, in fact, the wife is not being coy or unco-operative. She is merely adhering to the norm of non-commitalness [this being important in Malagasy society] . . . "If you don't come after dinner, you won't catch him" does not commit the speaker to the claim that if you do come after dinner you will catch him. . . . If you show up after dinner and he isn't there, you have no grounds for feeling that you had been given incorrect information.

A second example from Keenan and Ochs concerns the function of requesting—an area where there are great differences between language groups. The Westerner in Malagasy society may often find himself as having been understood to have made a request where in fact none was intended. For example, on one occasion, Edward [an American] in making idle conversation with a neighbour, happened to remark on the large pile of sweet potatoes in front of the man's house. About twenty minutes later, having returned to our own house, we were surprised to see the man's son appear with a plate of two cooked sweet potatoes! On reflection, it was clear that our casual remark was interpreted as a request by our neighbour.

Another area where there are great differences from one society to another is that of greeting. In English we often follow our initial greeting with a question like "How are you?" expecting a reply such as "Fine, thanks." A student from a speech community which does not have this convention will need to be taught it, otherwise he is likely to take the question at face value and respond with a lengthy report on the state of his health. The English speaker is likely to make a similar mistake in a speech community where a different type of question conventionally followed the greeting. In Japanese for example (according to Condon and Yousef, 1975) it is conventional to ask "Where are you going?" which receives the stereotyped answer "just over there."

It is worth noting in passing that we need to teach when *not* to use the "How are you?" question as well as when it is appropriate. Since it may trigger off a fairly lengthy sequence ("Oh, I'm fine thanks, and you?" "Yes, I'm OK.") it is inappropriate when meeting someone whom one perhaps meets often, in any situation where there is no time to stop and talk. Students who always trigger off such sequences by invariably following "Hello" with "How are you?" can be extremely time consuming.

Differences like these, which are most apparent in what Halliday calls the "interpersonal" use of language, do not only occur between societies which have little in common (though it is of course here that the differences are most obvious). In fact between societies with common traditions there is the additional danger of "false friends" where the foreigner who comes from a "similar" culture is lulled into a false confidence over the way he uses language.

The Feasibility of Teaching Language Use

A further set of objections commonly raised against a communicative approach to language teaching claims that it is impossible (rather than unnecessary) to teach the rules of use. One argument is that these rules are so complex that any attempt to teach them is bound to end in failure. Even when the linguist is able to formulate rules for areas of language use, these are often so complex that they cannot easily be conveyed to students. The argument is a persuasive one; sociolinguistics is full of examples of the kinds of complexities which attempt to analyse areas of language use reveal. To illustrate these complexities we need only look at one small area of language use—forms of address for example. Brown and Gilman (1960) analyse the use of singular pronouns of address in a variety of languages. Many languages have two such pronouns. French has "tu" and "vous", German "du" and "Sie", Italian "tu" and "lei". Brown and Gilman refer to these pronouns generically as T ("tu", "du", etc.) and V ("vous", "Sie", etc.). Two major factors, they claim, affect the choice of T or V by a native speaker. One they call "power". Thus a superior may address an inferior with the T form, while the inferior uses V to his superior. The second factor is "solidarity". Speakers who see themselves as being similar in some way tend to use T to each other, while speakers who feel themselves dissimilar (in ways not related to power) both use V.

If we consider these two factors alone, we find that the rules governing use of T or V are indeed complex. A given speaker may find himself in no less than six kinds of relationships with others:

1. His "similar" superior.
2. His "dissimilar" superior.
3. His "similar" equal.
4. His "dissimilar" equal.

5. His "similar" inferior.
6. His "dissimilar" inferior.

In fact in two of these relationships the criteria of "power" and "solidarity" are in conflict, and suggest different pronoun usage.

If we then go on to consider how these T and V forms interact with other forms of address, then the full complexity of the situation is revealed. In English, as in many other languages, our choice of the name we use to refer to someone is affected by considerations like those of "power" and "solidarity". According to the situation we may call our employer "Dr. Smith", "John Smith", "John", "Johnny", and in some languages forms approximating to "Dr. John" and "Mr. Dr." could be added to this list. If we are expected to see him as a superior we might use "Dr. Smith" while he might address us, as his inferior, by our first name or by the surname without "Mr." If we regard him (or, as is more often the case, if he lets us regard him) as someone who shares the same office, does the same kind of work, and is in various ways "similar" to us, we might address him by first name also. In many languages the T/V distinction combines with the choice of names to create an extremely complex system of address. In Serbo-Croat, for example, two individuals may indicate "solidarity" by using first names; but may at the same time signal a difference of "power" by means of the T/V distinction—the inferior using V to the superior and the superior using T to the inferior. In other situations it will be the choice of names which indicates a power difference, while the T/V distinction expresses the solidarity relationship.

The rules governing the correct choice of address form are, then, highly complex. Nor has this area been chosen because of its exceptional difficulty. Any area of language use will contain similar complexities, some of which have been unravelled by linguists, many of which have not.[2] Teaching language use is certainly a daunting task, but this does not make it any the less necessary. It remains true that the student who does not know the rules of use—how to address someone, how to greet, to invite, to give advice, etc.—cannot communicate effectively in the foreign language.

We should also not forget that if we read recent literature (especially from the transformational school) on the analysis of such apparently simple structures as tag questions, negation, pronouns, conjunctions and many more, we might come to the conclusion that grammar also is too complex to teach. Yet no-one would use this as an argument against grammar teaching. All language teachers recognise that the process of teaching grammar, especially at the lower levels, involves making gross oversimplifications. As the students progress, so they are gradually introduced into the complexities of language structure. But the stage is never reached where the structural teaching does anything like justice to the complexities of grammar as they are seen by the linguist. If the language teacher were daunted by the complexities associated with every area of language, he would certainly give up the ghost very early in his career.

It is certainly true that *more is known* about grammar than about language use. Generations of linguists have explored every remote corner of the language system, while there are large areas of language use which remain uncharted territory. But if language teachers were in the habit of refusing to teach any aspect of language until the linguist had fully described it—eliminating all problems and uncertainties—the history of language teaching would indeed be short.[3]

The Desirability of Teaching Language Use

Another set of objections claims neither that we need not, nor that we cannot, but that we *should* not teach language use. These objections are based on the fact that there are differences in the ways people use language, and that these reflect differences in personality. If we wish to teach our student to invite, introduce, complain, apologise (and so on) we must naturally first select which ways of doing these things it is appropriate to teach. But by selecting in this way, the argument runs, we are imposing norms of behaviour on the student. We control not just what he says, but *who he is*. If for example we teach him to invite using the form "Would you care to . . .?", and to say "I'm awfully pleased to meet you" when introduced, then we are teaching him to be a particular kind of person—the kind of (what some would consider) somewhat affected person who says these things. Students often realise this, and are vocal in their objections. One student, when asked under what circumstances she would use the invitation form ". . . requests the pleasure of the company of . . . to a reception to be held. . . ." replied "Never, not even to the Queen of England." The formality of the invitation, and what appeared to her to be its deference, clearly offended her. Why should she learn to be the kind of formal, deferent person who writes this sort of thing? Other forms which students sometimes object to are those such as "Would you mind . . .?" used to make requests 'as in "Would you mind opening the window?"). Students translate them literally into their mother tongue, again find them over-formal and deferent, and openly refuse to use them. They object to having a deferent, formal personality thrust upon them.

The question of norms does of course arise in traditional language teaching, particularly as regards a pronunciation model, and the issue has generated much discussion in the past. But most native speakers we would even consider as a model use the vast majority of grammatical structures in roughly the same way regardless of social and personality differences. The question of norms is therefore not nearly so acute as it is when we take the teaching of language use as our aim.

What is the answer? To say that because of student objections like the ones above we should not attempt to teach language use is surely not right. Interestingly, if we ask what form the objecting students would use instead of "Would you mind . . .?" the answer is, more often than not, the imperative. "Would you mind opening the window?" is replaced by "Open the window, please." They wish to sound informal and non-deferent, but in many situations succeed only in sounding rude— conveying to the speaker an impression which they almost certainly do not wish to convey. We might almost say that it is their ignorance of "rules of use" that is thrusting a personality on them.

However personal our use of language, it *is* controlled by rules which every native speaker knows. One such rule (put crudely) says: "If you want to make a polite request in English, you can use "*Would you mind* . . .".; if you wish to be very direct, or even rude, you can use the imperative." It is a rule that the student should know; but by teaching it we are not thrusting a personality on him. Our duty is to tell him what impression he will convey by using such and such a form, but it is for him to decide which impression in a given situation he wishes to convey. The teacher tells the student *how* to be rude or polite; the student decides *whether* to be rude or polite.

This paper has considered objections to the teaching of language use.

These objections or variants of them re-occur in later sections of the book, where they are not always so easily dismissed. But usually the objections suggest modifications (though sometimes quite drastic ones) in the way we might best go about the task of teaching use. The basic premises that the task needs to, can and should be attempted remain largely unaffected.[4]

Notes

1. Widdowson (1978a and elsewhere) makes this point using the imperative as his example.
2. Another area is briefly touched on in Paper 7, page 96.
3. In this section we have considered whether the task of teaching language use should be attempted. The same points may be made in consideration of a slightly different question: whether or not "categories of language use" should be used as the basis for syllabus design. See Papers 11 and 19.
4. Note 3 above illustrates the kind of context in which such objections re-occur. See also Paper 7.

Paper 3:

The Semantic Syllabus Inventory

Part 1: Categories of Signification and Use

PAPERS 1 and 2 have considered what we should teach our students. The answer has so far been made in the most general terms: apart from structure and signification, it has been said, we should also teach "language use". But if this specification of aims is to be of any value to course designers and teachers, it has to be stated more precisely. If we sit down with the idea of designing a course or preparing a series of lessons, we need at the very least some specific statement of the areas (or "items") of language use that we wish to teach.

It is useful to think of the process by which we decide on specific teaching content as having two stages. At the first we draw up a list, or an inventory, of all the items we wish to teach. This list of items is the *syllabus inventory*. Then, as a second operation, we make various decisions about the presentation of these items, one of the most important concerning the order in which they will appear in the course. The result is a *syllabus*, which we might think of as being an "organised syllabus inventory". This paper will consider some of the issues involved in producing a syllabus inventory to take account of the need to teach language use. Paper 4 looks at aspects of the second stage—turning the syllabus inventory into a syllabus.

"Items" on the Syllabus Inventory

What is an "item"? In Paper 1 we looked at part of a traditional syllabus. The items appearing on this list are language structures. Item 3, for example, is the structural sequence *definite article + noun +*

"*is*" + *adjective*, and one of the illustrative sentences for this structure is "The car is new." The present continuous tense is introduced as Item 9, in the form *subject + verb + "-ing" + adverbial phrase* (illustrated by sentences like "He's sitting on my chair.", "He's standing on the floor."). The complete syllabus inventory for a general English course will naturally be a fairly lengthy affair. It will include most or all of the tenses, and a variety of sentence types—complex sentences with adverbial clauses of purpose, compound sentences with co-ordinating conjunctions, conditional sentences, and very many others. It will also contain a vocabulary list—the lexical items to be taught on the course. If we ask where the course designer gets his list of structural items from, the answer is the linguist. It is the linguist who provides the "original inventory" in the form of a structural description of the language, and from this description the course designer selects those structures he wishes to teach. The linguist also provides the terminology used in drawing up a traditional syllabus inventory. Terms like "possessive", "adverbial phrase", "uncountable noun" used in the same syllabus in Paper 1 are all taken from the linguist, for whom they have precise meanings.

A syllabus inventory lists the items we wish to teach. If we believe that the task of learning a language is mainly one of mastering language structures (and their signification), then the items on the inventory will, of course, be language structures. In the recent past syllabus inventories expressed in structural and lexical terms have become the norm; and, as noted in Paper 1, they have all come to look extremely alike. If we ask how these syllabuses reflect the aim of teaching signification, then the answer is a rather indirect one. In most cases the syllabus designer does not have to specify that signification needs to be taught, since there is an implicit understanding that the signification of each structure appearing on the inventory needs to be made clear to the student. But the need to teach signification will at times play a more explicit part in the construction of the syllabus. For example, items of similar or contrasting signification (like "for" and "since") will often be treated in sequence, so that the teacher may compare and contrast them in terms of signification as well as formal properties. And sometimes it will be clear from looking at a syllabus that at a given place the main teaching point is concerned with signification. *Present continuous vs. simple present* is an item that appears on many syllabuses, and it is certain that the lesson dealing with this item would concentrate on the differences in signification between the two structures.[1]

In the past, then, syllabus inventories have reflected the aims of teaching structure and (in a more indirect way) signification. But what if we wish to devise a syllabus with a communicative dimension—one that teaches language use as well as the language sytem? What items will our inventory then include? The "systemic" inventory lists language structures. In the same way the "communicative" inventory has to find some means of listing language uses—of "itemising" the uses to which our students will wish to put the language. But whereas the "systemic" course designer can turn to the linguist to derive both his list of structures and the terminology in which to express it, the "communicative" course designer has no such resources to fall back on. There is no ready-made description of language use, expressed in a precise and well-formulated terminology.

Functional and Semantico-Grammatical Categories

In 1971 the Council of Europe convened a team of experts whose brief it was to consider the feasibility of developing a language teaching system suitable for teaching all the languages used in the Council's member countries. One member of that team, D. A. Wilkins, had the particular task of developing a system of categories by means of which it would be possible to specify the communicative needs of the adult learner working within a European context. Wilkins developed two types of category, which he described in an article entitled "The linguistic and situational content of the common core in a unit/credit system" (Wilkins, 1973). Since these categories play an important part in the development of "communicative" syllabus inventories, it is worth looking at them in some detail.

One type of category is what he calls the "category of communicative function". A communicative function is, in the most general terms, a "use to which the language may be put". In his article, Wilkins gives a list of "functions" (as they may be called for short), and this list amounts to an exploratory attempt to "itemise" the areas of language use felt to be important for a particular group of students—in this case adult European learners. Here are some examples of functions taken at random from Wilkins' list: greeting; expressing sympathy; expressing disapproval; warning; inviting; requesting and giving information; agreeing; disagreeing.

In fact Wilkins divides his functions into eight categories. These are given in Table 1, together with examples.[2]

TABLE 1

1. Modality
   E.g. expressing (degrees of) certainty, expressing necessity and conviction

2. Moral discipline and evaluation
   E.g. expressing approval and disapproval

3. Suasion
   E.g. persuading, suggesting, urging

4. Argument
   E.g. informing, arguing, asserting

5. Rational enquiry and exposition
   E.g. expressing implications, exemplifying, defining

6. Personal emotions
   E.g. expressing pleasure, astonishment, shock, annoyance

7. Emotional relations
   E.g. greeting, expressing gratitude

8. Interpersonal relations
   E.g. expressing degrees of formality and politeness

Wilkins provides lists of representative functions for each of these eight areas. Table 2 shows the functions occurring under the heading of SUASION. The column on the right gives examples of the language items associated with some functions.

Wilkins calls his second type of category the "semantico-grammatical". The following examples are again taken from Wilkins (1973): duration, frequency, quantity, dimension, location.

TABLE 2 (from Wilkins, 1973)

Suasion	
i.e. utterances designed to influence others	1. Suggestion Let's go to the zoo. We could go to the zoo. Shall we go to the zoo? (I suggest a visit to the zoo.) that we go to the zoo.)
1. Suasion — persuade, suggest, advise, recommend, advocate, exhort, beg, urge, propose	
2. Prediction — warning, caution, menace, threat, (prediction), instruction, direction, invitation	1. Warning (comprehension only?) Be careful! Look out! Mind the puddle! . . . . (If you don't go, you may miss the last bus.)
	2. Direction (comprehension only?) Take a 73 bus to Oxford Street and get off at Oxford Circus. Or take a taxi. You'll have to . . . . Telephone instructions, etc.
	3. Invitation (comprehension only?) Would you like to have a drink? How about a drink? Have a drink, won't you? Won't you have a drink? (Can I persuade you to have a drink?)

Each of these concepts has a variety of grammatical features associated with it. The concept of duration, for example, is associated grammatically with prepositions like "for" (indicating the period of time that something lasted), "since" (indicating the point of time when something began), and "from . . . to" 'which specifies duration by saying when something began and ended). But a concept of duration can also be expressed by verb tense. An idea of "limited duration" is often expressed by choice of the present continuous as opposed to the simple present tense. Sentences like "He is reading Shakespeare.", "He is making a lot of money.", He is living in London." usually give the idea that what is happening is of limited duration. "He reads Shakespeare.", "He makes a lot of money." and "He lives in London.", on the other hand, suggest that the actions have gone on (and may continue) for a long time.

Wilkins lists six main areas into which his semantico-grammatical categories fall. *Frequency, duration, sequence* and *age* are some of the concepts associated with TIME. QUANTITY is the second area which covers numerals, and quantifiers like "all", "a lot of", "some", "no". The concepts of *dimension, location* and *motion* come under the general heading of SPACE. The fourth area is called by Wilkins MATTER. It is the least developed of the six areas, and covers the ways in which "the learner wants to refer to the 'physical' world". The area is dropped in Wilkins' later model (1976), perhaps indicating some dissatisfaction with it. A large number of concepts are expressed in language by means of CASE relations (the fifth area). The *agentive* case for example is used to express the initiator of an action, and in English is usually associated with the subject position in an active sentence. "The person to whom an action is done" is a rough description of the concept which is expressed by use of the *dative* case, which in English is generally signalled by an indirect object (as in "Give *John* the ticket."), or a prepositional phrase ("Give the ticket *to John*."). Wilkins' final major area is called DEIXIS. Deixis is concerned with the means languages use to relate utterances to their context. For example, one use of the personal pronouns is to express the concept of "someone mentioned before". If we hear someone say "Peter has a new coat. He bought it only last week.", we will certainly (unless given evidence to the contrary) identify the "he" of the second sentence with the "Peter" of the first. Here the personal pronoun is being used to relate the second sentence to its linguistic context—the preceding utterance "Peter has a new coat." Some types of deixis relate utterances to a context which is non-linguistic. For example, the adverbials "here" and "there" are used to indicate location in relation to the speaker. In general terms "here" refers to some point near the speaker, while "there" refers to a point at some distance.

The Difference between Semantico-Grammatical and Functional Categories

What is the difference between these "semantico-grammatical categories", and the "categories of communicative function"? In what way is a concept like *frequency* (or *expressing frequency*) different from a function like *sympathy* (or *expressing sympathy*)? The key lies in the distinction, suggested in Paper 1, between "signification" and "use". The semantico-grammatical categories provide a means of "itemising signification", while functions are "items of use". In Paper 2 the sentence "You will come tomorrow." was analysed in terms of the signification of its constituent parts. We noted that the signification of "will" was to indicate future time, while "tomorrow" signified "the day following today". An alternative way of expressing this is to say that "will" indicates a concept of futurity, "tomorrow" the concept of "a point of (future) time". The analysis was a semantico-grammatical one. But, as we saw, this analysis told us nothing of the *uses* to which the sentence might be put, of the various *functions* it might perform. These include issuing a command, reassuring, or even expressing resignation. One recognises the function of an utterance by asking why the speaker said it. In the case of the computer's sentence the answer might be "to tell the person to come tomorrow" or (in more general terms) to "issue a command". The answer would *not* be "to express future time". There is indeed a concept of futurity contained in the sentence, but the sentence was not uttered in order to express this concept.

A Terminological Issue

In this discussion of "semantico-grammatical categories", the word "concept" has been used a lot. We have spoken of the "concept" of duration, the "concept" of frequency, the "concept" of dimension. Another word which expresses the same idea is the word "notion". In fact van Ek (of the Council of Europe team) and others use the word "notion" as a convenient way of referring to "semantico-grammatical category", just as we have used "function" as an abbreviation for "category of communicative function". But unfortunately the term notion, and even more the adjective "notional" have come to be used in another sense, and this has led to considerable confusion. Wilkins and others speak of "notional syllabuses", meaning syllabuses which are based on an inventory which lists *both* functions *and* semantico-grammatical items. The implications here is that "notion" is an "umbrella term" covering both types of category. These two uses of the word "notion" can be clarified by means of a diagram:

TABLE 3

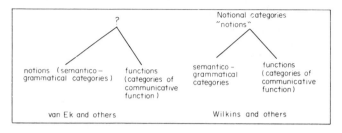

This book will follow van Ek's use of the word "notion", meaning a semantico-grammatical category. In this usage *duration, frequency* and *dimension* are "notions". When we need an umbrella term to refer to a syllabus which, in contrast to the structural syllabus, uses notions and functions as its starting point, we shall speak of a "semantic syllabus".

Teaching Signification

It has already been noted that syllabus designers and teachers have always been aware of the need to teach signification. When the teacher makes the distinction between the present continuous and the simple present he inevitably refers to notions—such as *frequency* ("habitual action" being often associated with the simple present), *duration* ("limited duration" can, as noted earlier, be expressed by use of the present continuous) and *contiguity* (the present continuous being used for an action taking place while the speaker is talking). Similarly, in his explanation of the signification of "for" and "since", the teacher would doubtless draw a distinction between the notion of a "point of time" ("since *February*", "since *last week*") and the notion of a "period of time" ("for *two weeks*", "for *a year*"). There is nothing new about the idea of notions.

What *is* new is that no one has ever been very systematic about notions. We may *refer* to notions in our grammar teaching; but we have never organised a course around them, and we rarely enter the classroom with the aim of giving systematic coverage to a particular notional area. We may talk about the notion of frequency in our lesson on the present continuous—but the subject of our lesson is "the present continuous", not "the notion of frequency". Still less has anyone attempted to identify the key areas of signification that a group of students will want to master. It is in this sense that Wilkins' semantico-grammatical category provides the possibility of a new approach.

Part 2: The Needs Analysis Principle

There is an immense range of notions and functions which the native speaker will regularly use language to perform during the course of his everyday life. This suggests that any attempt to predict all the possible notional and functional uses to which the foreign learner might wish—in all possible circumstances—to put the language he is learning, will result in an absurdly long list, quite impracticable for teaching purposes. If we are to produce a syllabus inventory of reasonable proportions, we must therefore develop some criterion for selecting these notions and functions which our particular group of learners will find especially useful. These may then be taught to the exclusion of other, less necessary, ones.

How can the particularly useful notions and functions be identified? This is a question which the Council of Europe team, particularly Richterich (1973) and van Ek (1975), has attempted to answer by looking closely at the "language needs" of groups of learners. Language needs are "the requirements which arise from the use of a language in the multitude of situations which may arise in the social lives of individuals and groups" (Richterich, 1973, p. 32). By analysing the language needs of specific groups of learners, we should be able to identify those notions and functions it will be most valuable to teach.

In order to explore some of the issues involved in the analysis of language needs, we shall look at the cases of two individuals who are learning English for specific reasons. To narrow the scope of discussion we shall deal with functions only, though what will be said will apply to notions as well.

Hans and Elke are a German couple. Hans is a lawyer specialising in international law, and in the course of his work he is often involved in dealing with people from abroad. Indeed, on several occasions he has even attended court cases abroad where the language being used was English. Elke works as a secretary for a large export company. Her boss is always travelling to meetings abroad, often in England, and when this happens Elke sometimes has to travel ahead of him to make arrangements for his stay. Which functions would it be most useful to teach Elke for this part of her job? *Making requests for information* will certainly be an important one. It is her job to find out about plane and train times, to request information about where meetings are to be held, when they are due to begin, what is on the agenda. Other functions which we might predict she will regularly have to perform include *making bookings and appointments, greeting, expressing gratitude, confirming arrangements.* And if we look at the list of 'suasive functions" in Table 2, there will undoubtedly be some there which she might find useful—*suggestions, advising, recommending, inviting,* for example.

There are other functions on that list which, though she may conceivably need them at one time or another, are nevertheless of less potential use. *Exhort, beg, urge, menace, instruct* are possible candidates. Looking beyond suasive functions at the list in general, it is unlikely that in the normal course of duty she will be required to *define, scorn, contend* or *protest,* for example, in English.

By looking in this way at how we predict Elke will want to use her English, we may arrive at a manageable list of functions to be taught. Note that this list will be different from one drawn up along similar lines for her husband Hans. *His* language needs are quite different, and in fact many of the functions which are relatively unimportant for Elke will be of prime importance to him. Some of the functions mentioned above are cases in point. For Hans the lawyer, the ability to *define, scorn, contend, protest* (as well as *exhort, beg, urge, menace, instruct*) are essential tricks of the trade, and he will want to be taught how to do these things in English. Similarly, functions important to Elke, like *making bookings* and *asking about train times,* may be of relatively little use to Hans.

The Concept of the Common Core

Secretaries, then, have different language needs from lawyers, and needs analysis provides us with the means of arriving at a manageable list of notions and functions for teaching purposes. Indeed, it is one of the great advantages of this approach that it enables us to discriminate between various learner types, and to produce syllabus inventories (and courses) specifically geared to their needs. But this advantage brings with it a problem. As long as we are dealing with groups having the same needs, the system works well. If we are lucky enough to be teaching a group of secretaries or lawyers, then the analysis of language needs is a feasible proposition. But most teachers are not in this position. Often, at the adult level, they are dealing with groups of students each of whom wishes to use the language in quite dissimilar ways. The teacher whose class contains Elke the secretary, Hans the lawyer (and perhaps a doctor, an engineer and a mechanic as well) has this problem. It is compounded by the fact that probably many of the students just do not have a specific purpose in learning English. They are learning it for fun, to talk to people (though they may not be too sure exactly to whom), or just to pass an examination. The teacher of children is in a similar predicament. She has no way of predicting how her students might wish to use their English. Some may, when older, decide to be secretaries, some lawyers, others doctors, engineers and mechanics. The only thing that *is* certain is that each child will eventually need his or her English for a different purpose—assuming (as the teacher cannot with certainty) that each child will in fact need English at all in the future.

The Council of Europe team met this problem in an extreme form. They were concerned with developing a framework for teaching languages to the most general and vague of audiences—the average adult European, living in any of a number of countries, wishing to learn any of a number of languages for any of a number of purposes. Because it has to cater for such a wide variety of students working in so many different environments, a chief prerequisite of the framework is clearly that it should be highly flexible. For this reason the team developed what they call a "unit/credit" system. In this system, areas of language use are divided into "units". Since different areas of use will be relevant to the needs of different groups of learners according to their specific requirements, the students are guided into a choice of which "units" to cover. Credits are given for units completed and when a number of credits have been gained, a qualification is given. Thus qualification can be obtained "in a variety of ways appropriate to varying . . . patterns of study and needs" (Trim, 1973, p. 18).

The aspect of this system most relevant to the present discussion is the concept of the "common core". The team recognised that there will be areas of interest common to all students, whatever their particular situations and specialisations. Thus there will be a "common core" of functions relevant to secretary as much as engineer, to doctor as much as mechanic. This might include such functions as *greeting, introducing, inviting, asking for information*—functions associated with the general area of "social life", rather than with any particular occupation. It seems reasonable to assume that all students (adults and children) will need to be able to do such things in the foreign language. Each learning level in the Council of Europe's unit/credit system will have a *common core* of units, alongside other specialised units which the students select to study according to their specific interest.

Part 3: The Framework for Needs Analysis

The Concept of Situation[3]

If our notional and functional lists are to avoid being confused and arbitrary, our needs analysis must take place within a framework. In order to consider a possible framework we shall imagine that we have a group of "Elkes"—students, that is, whose need for English involves use of the language on business trips to Britain. How, we shall ask, might we set about producing a syllabus inventory for these students?

In the quotation on page 40, Richterich speaks of the requirements arising in the "multitude of situations" the individual will find himself in. If we are able to ascertain in exactly which situations Elke will want to use English, this will provide us with a principled framework for preparing our notional/functional lists. But what is a "situation"? One dictionary[4] defines it as a "set of circumstances", and van Ek (thinking of "situations" specifically in relation to language use) talks of "the complex of extra-linguistic conditions which determines the nature of a language-act" (1973). The words "set" and "complex" are important here, because they convey the idea that there are a large number of factors which go to make up a "situation". We shall explore what these factors are, and how they relate to the analysis of language needs by means of an example.

Topic

It has already been said that *requesting information* is a function Elke will find useful. Here are two requests for information she is likely to make:

1. Could you please tell me the times of flights from London to Manchester?
2. I'd like to know how much a single room costs for the night, please.

Compare these with the following two sentences, also *requests for information*:

3. Could you please tell what time the lecture begins?
4. I'd like to know where the football stadium is, please.

Sentences (3) and (4) are unlikely to be useful to Elke because they are *about* things which would not interest her professionally; their *topics* (lectures and football stadia—or, in more general terms, education and sport) are outside her sphere of professional interest. The *topics* of (1) and (2) are (again in broad terms) "travel" and "accommodation". These are of direct interest to her and there are areas of vocabulary (and even perhaps characteristic structures) associated with each which she will want to know. Other topic areas of potential interest to Elke will include that of *personal identification*. She will certainly need to be able to give her name, the address and telephone number of her hotel, to describe where she comes from and what her job is. She will also want to know about certain types of *services*, such as post, telephone, bank. During the course of her stay in England she may have to enquire how much it costs to send letters, to ask for stamps; and she will want to know about Britain's first and second class postal system. She will also certainly make telephone calls, and must know expressions like "engaged", "operator", "STD" associated with the "language of telephones". Talking about cheques, money drafts, postal orders, etc., will probably also be things she finds it necessary to do.

Van Ek (1975) notes that [the learner will have to do more than fulfil . . . general language functions. He will not only have to give information in the abstract, but he will want to give information about something; he will wish to express certainty or uncertainty with respect to something; he will want to apologise for something. The answers to these questions—"About what?", "With respect to what?", "for what?" will identify the topics which will interest Elke and her group.

Setting

A second aspect of situation we need to consider concerns not *what* is talked about, but *where* it is said. Compare these sentences with the original (1) and (2):

5. Tower to 272. Can we have your ETA, please?
6. Baker's Travel here. Can you give me a price on singles, high season, no bath or shower, please?

The four sentences are similar as regards function and general topic, but sentences (5) and (6) are unlikely to be of interest to Elke's group, because these students will probably not find themselves in the kinds of place (or *settings*) where these sentences would be uttered. (5) is probably spoken in an airport control room—the authorities are asking an airline crew for its expected time of arrival (ETA)—and (6) might be a request made to a hotel by a tour operator. It would be uttered in the tour operator's office. Elke will want to learn the "language of the airport information desk" and the "language of the hotel foyer" (likely settings for sentences (1) and (2)), but not the "language of the airport control room" or the "language of the tour operator's office".

In the most general terms "setting" means geographical region, and the first question we need to ask concerns the country where our students will use their English. Is it a country in which English is the native language; or where an accepted variety of English is used as the second language; or a non-English speaking country where English is used as a lingua franca? The answers to these questions will certainly affect the kind of English we teach our students—the pronunciation we offer them as a model, the words (and even the structures) we ask them to learn.

In fact syllabus designers in the past have become used to asking this kind of question about geographical region, and do often make the answers affect the actual content of their courses. But it is rarer to find more detailed questions asked about setting. In precisely what locations are the students likely to use their English? In the street? The house? Shops? Kitchen? Hotel? Railway station? TV studio? School? Office? Airport control tower? The answers to such questions are important because they affect the choice of language items appropriate to teach the student group. In the case of Elke's group we might predict that some of the above settings—like house, kitchen, TV studio, school, airport control tower—are likely to be irrelevant. But others—street, hotel, railway station and office perhaps—will be important.

Role

Topic is concerned with *what*, and setting with *where*. A third important question concerns *who*. Here are two more sentences:

7. Hi, George. Give me the London to Manchester times, will you?
8. Would you kindly inform me of the price of a single room for one night?

These sentences are similar to the original two—(1) and (2)—in all respects so far considered. They are functionally identical, all being requests for information; their topics are the same (travel and accommodation), and they can certainly be uttered in the same settings— airport information desk and hotel foyer. But again, (7) and (8) are likely to be less use to Elke than (1) and (2). The respect in which the two pairs of sentences differ concerns the *roles* which the speakers are adopting or, in other terms, the *role relationships* holding between speaker and listener. Sentences (1) and (2) are the sorts of sentences uttered by strangers; the role relationship is one of "stranger to stranger". The speaker and listener in (7) are clearly friends, the role relationship therefore being "friend to friend". In the case of (8), there are several possible role relationships involved. The sentence may possibly be uttered by someone who is extremely haughty and formal, and in this case the role relationship being implied by the speaker is "superior to subordinate". More feasibly, it might be uttered by someone who is simply irritated. He has perhaps asked for the information several times and not received it. His patience is wearing thin. In this case we might best characterise the speaker's role in "psychological" rather than "social" terms. He is, we might say, adopting a role of hostility or antipathy towards the listener.

As with functions, notions, topics and settings, the roles we teach our students to fulfil will depend on their language needs. Thus managers learning English may wish to know how to address subordinates appropriately, while for secretaries like Elke the correct form for addressing superiors will be important. In general terms such role relationships may be specified as "superior to subordinate" and "subordinate to superior"; more specifically we may use terms like "manager to assistant", "secretary to manager", "customer to tradesman", "private person to official", and so on. Relationships of the solidarity as well as the power type must also be considered. Some students will wish to use the language predominantly to communicate with friends ("friend to friend" role relationship) while for others the "stranger to stranger" relationship is more important. We may also list some of the *psychological roles* our students will wish to perform, by use of terms like "respect", "obedience", "affection", "sympathy", "antipathy".

It is important to note how the factors considered here relate to the concept of "appropriateness" discussed in Paper 1. There it was pointed out that a fundamental aim of communicative language teaching is to teach the student appropriateness. If we ask "appropriate to what?", part of the answer is of course "appropriate to the *situations* in which they are using language". Now that the concept of situation has been broken down somewhat, we may answer this question in a more specific way by saying that the students' language must be appropriate to the *topic* they are dealing with, the *setting* they are operating in, and the *role* they wish to fulfil.

Activity Types in the Four Skills

Having identified the situations Elke will wish to use her language in, we may turn our attention to what she will have to *do* in these situations. In the first instance we may consider her likely activities in terms of the four skills—speaking, listening, reading and writing. As regards reading and writing, in the area of social life she will probably want to read newspapers during her stay in Britain, and in settings like those of street, shop, hotel she will come across a variety of signs and notices—giving her information on where to go, what to do, how to do it, how much things cost, and so on. Her writing needs in social life will probably be few. She may find herself in a situation where she needs to reply in writing to formal invitations, and perhaps she will also want to write letters to friends. Writing tasks connected with her work are likely to be more.

Situations are sure to arise in connection with the office setting where she will have to write various communications on business topics—letters, minutes, memos, telegrams and perhaps even reports. All these she will probably also have to read and, at least, as far as her work is concerned, her reading and writing needs are likely to be similar.

It is not difficult to predict many of Elke's speaking and listening activities related to the listed topics, settings and roles. They include such activities as (in the hotel setting) checking in, finding out about meal times, paying the bill; buying tickets, asking about timetables (in railway stations, airports, travel agencies); asking for directions, taking taxis (in the street); and, in shops—asking where various departments are, trying clothes on, buying things . . . and paying for them. The list could be extended, and, after we have looked at her business as well as her social needs, it will certainly be a long one.

One thing which this cursory look at some areas of Elke's language needs reveals is that in a sense we are involved in producing four syllabus inventories, rather than one—for each of the four language skills. To what extent will these inventories be different? In some areas they will be quite dissimilar. It may, for example, be part of Elke's job to attend business meetings and take minutes. This activity has a large listening component and probably no speaking component at all; she has to understand what is said, but may not participate verbally herself. If we are to train Elke for this activity, the listening comprehension part of our syllabus inventory will have to include the functions which the speakers are likely to perform—describing financial arrangements, making plans for the future, issuing instructions perhaps, and many more. These functions may have no place in the spoken part of her inventory. On the other hand many of Elke's other listening needs will be in everyday situations where she herself also speaks, and often the kind of functions she performs—*greeting, making arrangements* and so on—will be those which her interlocutor also performs. To this extent her speaking and listening needs will overlap, and can be covered in a "joint" inventory. Likewise there will (as already noted) be many similarities between the reading and writing tasks she has to perform.

But there is one important difference between what Elke must be able to say and write, and what she must be able to understand. She will have to understand a range of English that is far greater than she can herself use. This is because whereas she can control what she produces, she has no such control over what others say or write to her. The British people Elke speaks to will certainly on occasions use expressions to *greet, invite, make arrangements, complain*, which are beyond her productive capacity. She must understand more than she can say, and this has two consequences for the syllabus inventory. Firstly it indicates the need to specify whether listed items are to be learned receptively (for listening or reading) or productively (for speaking or writing). Secondly it suggests that in many areas of the inventory there are likely to be many more items listed for receptive than for productive learning.

Despite any overlap in Elke's language needs as regards the four skills, it is important that we should approach the task of drawing up an inventory prepared to consider each of these skills separately. Such an approach is not characteristic of traditional procedures, where the tendency was to teach all the items on the syllabus in relation to all the four skills.

Activities, Functions, Notions and Exponents

The question considered in the previous section was "What is Elke likely to have to *do* in the various situations in which she uses English?" The answer was made in terms of a number of "activities", looked at in relation to the four language skills. A possible next stage is to consider what functions these activities involve. We might take the activity of "checking in at the hotel" as an example, and ask what functions are involved here. Elke will certainly have to know how to *request inform-ation*, in the first instance about the availability and cost of rooms, but also about a number of other matters—does the room have a shower or a bath?, does the hotel have a restaurant? She will also have to *give information*—about herself (what her full name is, where she is from), about the length of her stay, and so on. *Requesting services* is another function she will probably want to perform in relation to the "checking-in activity". Would the porter please take the suitcases to her room? Could she be woken at 7.00 the next morning? Can she deposit some valuables in the hotel safe? These are possible speaking activities associated with "checking in", and we would predict the associated listening activities in the same way.

When we have looked at each of the activities Elke is likely to perform, the result will be a list—systematically arrived at—of the functions it will be useful to teach her. Since the number of activities is great, the functional list will be long; but there will be considerable overlap, and many of the activities will involve a common core of recurring functions. The three mentioned here—*requesting information, giving information* and *requesting services*—are cases in point.

The procedure for arriving at a notional list is similar. It will be based on the specification of situations (topics, settings, roles) and of the activities Elke is likely to perform in these situations. As with functions, there will be a considerable common core of items associated with very many situations and activities, and this is likely to include items like *frequency, quantity, size* and *duration.* But there will be other notions with a more restricted application, and one way of categorising these is in terms of the topic list. Topic areas (*personal identification* and *travel* are two that have been mentioned earlier) have particular notions associated with them. *Personal identification,* for example, involves the expression of notions concerned with age, marital status, occupation, etc., while notions concerned with the expression of direction, destination, mode of transport, and so on, are associated with the area of *travel.*

As a final stage we list the structures associated with the notions and functions appearing on the inventory. The selection will be guided by the various aspects of situation we have discussed, and it has already been shown how these aspects will affect the selection of structures in relation to the function of requesting information.

It has become standard practice to refer to "a way in which a function is expressed" as that function's "exponent", and to say that such and such a structure is being used to "expound" such and such a function. Thus we would call the items on the right of Table 2 (page 36) "exponents" or "ways of expounding" the functional area of *suasion.*

The Threshold Level

In a paper discussing the aims of the Council's team, Trim (1973) notes that it is "common practice" to recognise five levels of language proficiency which he calls:

1. Threshold
2. Basic
3. General Competence
4. Advanced
5. Full Professional Standard

The team decided that it should be the Threshold Level to receive first priority, and van Ek was given the task of providing a common core syllabus inventory for this level. The finished specification appears in the form of a book called *The Threshold Level* (van Ek, 1975). Equivalents have since appeared for European languages other than English and a *Threshold Level for Schools* was produced by van Ek (1978). Van Ek (1973) defines the Threshold Level as "a minimum level of foreign language competence". It is a level "below which no further levels can be usefully distinguished". Later, however, it was decided that a lower level

TABLE 4

1. Specification of situations
    a. roles (social and psychological)
    b. settings
    c. topics

2. Language activities specified in terms of the four skills

3. Language functions

4. Notions
    a. related to particular topics
    b. general

5. Language forms specified according to:
    a. functions
    b. topic-related notions
    c. general notions

6. Degree of skill. How "well" the students must be able to
    speak, listen, write, read

would indeed be useful, and a specification known as *Waystage* (van Ek and Alexander, 1977) was therefore produced.

The procedure suggested by van Ek's Threshold Level is the one that has been described here, though he considers one further variable (degree of skill) which has not been discussed. This procedure is summarised in Table 4.

Since 1975 other needs analysis frameworks have been developed, the most complete (and complex) being Munby's (1978).

Notes

1. Some would claim a more central role for signification in the design of a syllabus by saying that the syllabus designer (perhaps unconsciously) introduces some "grading of signification". In other words he introduces structures with a more "complex" meaning after structures with a "simpler" meaning. "Complexity of meaning" is certainly one factor the syllabus designer would bear in mind.
2. These eight functional areas were later modified in Wilkins (1976).
3. The principle of studying language in relation to situation has a tradition especially in British linguistics, and different frameworks for analysing the concept of situation have been developed. Cf. Firth (1957) and Halliday, McIntosh and Strevens (1964).
4. *The Concise Oxford Dictionary of Current English*, ed. by Fowler, H. W. and Fowler, F. G., Oxford University Press.

Section 2:

SYLLABUS DESIGN

Paper 4:

Selecting Units of Organisation for a Semantic Syllabus

This paper was written to follow on from Paper 3, but may be read on its own. It has been placed in a different section because, whereas the previous papers cover ground already familiar to many readers, it considers a problem which has received less general attention. This is the problem of converting a syllabus inventory (the unordered series of lists specifying teaching content) into a syllabus which may form the basis for an actual teaching programme. The paper deals specifically with the selection of a unit of organisation for the syllabus. It considers possible criteria for selection and, in the final section, looks at the possibility of a "multi-dimensional syllabus"—one in which various units of organisation are used.

Possible Units of Organisation

WHEN we come to organise a semantic syllabus inventory[1] (of the Threshold Level type) into a syllabus, we face a problem that the structural syllabus designer never had to tackle. This is the problem of deciding what shall be taken as the *unit of organisation*. For the traditional syllabus designer there was never any question what this should be—it was the structure. Indeed, apart from lexis and perhaps phonemes, this is the only type of item his inventory contained, and the process of developing syllabus inventory into syllabus simply involved placing the structures into suitable order for teaching. But since the semantic inventory contains items of more than one type, the designer must select his unit of organisation, and it is the existence of this choice

55

that helps to make syllabus design one of the more interesting areas of language teaching today.

The designer may take as his unit of organisation any one of the item types listed on the inventory. He can organise the syllabus so that each teaching unit in his eventual coursebook covers one functional area (like *greeting, inviting*), and in this case we would say he had produced a "functional syllabus". Or he may arrange it so that each unit covers one setting (like *railway stations, the bank*). We would call this a setting-based syllabus. Similarly he could produce a notional, topic-based, or even conceivably a role-based syllabus. But just because we refer to these syllabus types using such labels, it does not follow that each syllabus type takes account of only one sort of item. If we produce a functional syllabus, for example, this does not imply that it is drawn up without consideration for the notions, topics, settings, roles, activities and structures listed on the inventory. These various item types constitute the total specification of teaching content. The label "functional syllabus" merely indicates that we are taking the function as our "unit of organisation".

An example will illustrate this important point. We shall imagine that, for the sake of exposition, we have an inventory containing only nine items—three functions, three settings and three notions. Any real inventory will naturally be far more complex, containing more items of different types (such as topic, role, structure); but for the purposes of exemplification nine items will suffice, and these are taken from van Ek (1975):

Functions

    1. Requesting information
    2. Giving information
    3. Enquiring how certain/uncertain something is

Settings

    1. Hotel
    2. Station
    3. Shop

Notions

    1. Availability/non-availability
    2. Location
    3. Cost

There are several ways in which we might set about preparing lessons to cover these items. One possibility would be to write three lessons, each dealing with one function; the first would therefore teach *requesting information*, the second *giving information* and the third *enquiring how certain/uncertain something is*. In each lesson we would ensure that the illustrative sentences and the sentences given for practice are all ones that could be used in a hotel, station or shop. In this way we would introduce language relevant to the three settings on the inventory. Similarly, we can ensure that the sentences involve notions of *availability/non-availability*, *location* and *cost*. Here for example are nine sentences which could be introduced in the first lesson, called "Requesting Information". The relevant settings and notions are given in brackets:

1. I'd like to know whether you have any single rooms free for tonight.
   (hotel; availability/non-availability)

2. Could you tell me whether there are any seats free for the 10.30 to Dover?
   (station; availability/non-availability)

3. Could you tell me whether you have any size 11 shoes in stock?
   (shop; availability/non-availability)

4. Could you tell me where the dining room is, please?
   (hotel; location)

5. Could you tell me where the ticket office is, please?
   (station; location)

6. Could you tell me where the shoe department is, please?
   (shop; location)

7. I'd like to know how much a single room costs.
   (hotel; cost)

8. Could you tell me what the single fare to London is, please?
   (station; cost)

9. I'd like to know how much this pair costs, please.
   (shop; cost).

Lessons 2 and 3 would deal in the same way with the functions of *giving information* and *enquiring how certain/uncertain* something is respectively. In each case the practice given would be concerned with availability, location and cost, in the hotel, station and shop settings.

These three lessons introduce language relevant to all the functions, settings and notions on our short inventory. But the unit of organisation is the function; each lesson deals with one function, and the link between the language introduced within the same lesson is a functional one. We might express the organisation of these three lessons in the form of a simple table:

1. Requesting information

    Settings: hotel, shop, station

    Notions: availability/non-availability, location, cost

2. Giving information

    Settings and notions as above

3. Enquiring about uncertainty/certainty

    Settings and notions as above

This table is in fact a short functional syllabus; it is an arrangement of all the items appearing on our syllabus inventory, placed in the order in which they are to be taught.

But there are other ways in which these functions, settings and notions could be covered. We might, for example, take the setting as our unit of organisation, and write three setting-based lessons. The first we could call "At the Hotel", the second "At the Station" and the third "In a Shop". Once again the lessons could be made to relate to all the functions and notions on the inventory. Lesson 1 would deal with requesting and giving information, and enquiring about certainty—in a hotel setting. The requests, enquiries and given information would concern such matters as the availability of hotel rooms, their location and cost. Similarly with lessons 2 and 3 for the other settings. Our short syllabus would this time be setting-based, and it would look like this:

1. At the Hotel

> Functions: requesting information, giving information, en-
> quiring about certainty/uncertainty
> Notions: availability/non-availability/uncertainty

2. At the Station

> Functions and notions as above

3. In a Shop

> Functions and notions as above

The third possibility would be to construct three lessons with a notional orientation. The syllabus would this time be notional, with this form:

1. Availability/non-availability

> Functions: requesting information, giving information, en-
> quiring about certainty/uncertainty
> Settings: hotel, station, shop

2. Location

> Functions and settings as above

3. Cost

> Functions and settings as above

There are, then, a variety of ways in which the items on the inventory may be covered. The example above has considered functional, setting-based and notional organisations only; it goes without saying that had the example inventory included other item types, these could have been made the unit of organisation as well.

At this point it is worth clarifying that since semantic syllabus inventories also include lists of structures, the structure also may be made the unit of organisation.[2] It is as easy (or, more to the point, just as difficult) to develop a structural syllabus out of an inventory of van Ek (1975) type as it is to develop any of the various semantic syllabus types.

But note that a structural syllabus derived from such an inventory is quite different in conception from a structural syllabus derived in the traditional way. The traditional structural syllabus aims eventually to cover all the structures of the language, and it systematically goes through these structures one by one. "It exists, therefore we must teach it." is the rationale. Since a semantic inventory is drawn up by a process of needs analysis, the rationale for any syllabus derived from it is "It is useful, therefore we must teach it."

Criteria for Selecting Unit of Organisation

How does the syllabus designer choose which of the various possible syllabus types to adopt? What criteria can he use, and what are the implications involved in selecting one or another mode of organisation? Since the course designer has not before had the kind of choice he is now faced with, these issues are new and deserve more attention than the literature has so far given them. In this section we shall consider some possible criteria for distinguishing between the various types of semantic syllabus.

i) Desired Focus of Teaching

A syllabus may be seen as a vehicle by means of which certain information is conveyed to the students and certain types of language practice are given. We therefore might expect different syllabus types to be better suited to giving different sorts of information and practice. If our main aim is to provide grammatical information and practice, then it is natural that we should choose the structural syllabus as our vehicle. By focusing in each lesson on a separate structure we are able to concentrate attention on structural problems and present the grammar of the language in an orderly progression. It is our perception of what it is important for the students to learn which leads us to select a particular type of syllabus.

There are situations in which this criterion—perception of what it is important for the students to learn—will lead to the choice of one or another semantic syllabus type. It may for example be that a predominant aim of the course is to convey cultural information. We may wish to teach the students about the British banking system, about British education, and so on. This type of information could of course be conveyed within any syllabus type. If we adopt a functional syllabus design, for example, one of the units may well cover the function of *requesting services*. One of the sentences appearing in this unit might be "I'd like to open a bank account, please." The point in the lesson where this sentence is introduced provides the opportunity to discuss the various types of bank account it is possible to open. In fact it would be possible at that point to launch into a full-scale consideration of British banking.

But there are two reasons why this solution is unsatisfactory. Firstly, the functional nature of the lessons will soon be undermined. It is certain that the *requesting services* unit will contain sentences appropriate to other settings. Apart from "I'd like to open a bank account." it might also contain "I'd like to have my car serviced." (in the garage setting) and "I'd like to send a telegram to Turin." (in the Post Office setting). Like banking, British garages and the postal service might well be subjects we wish to pursue at length. In this situation the lesson which started out dealing with *requesting services* will turn into an information-giving session dealing with banks, garages and the postal services.

The second reason is that sessions like these are unlikely to do adequate justice to the cultural information we wish to convey. Banks, garages and the post may well be *mentioned* in the lesson on *requesting services*, but it will almost certainly not be possible to convey all the desired information in that lesson. It may also prove difficult over the course as a whole—organised as it is in a functional way—to deal with the settings in the required detail. Then there is the question of uneven distribution. Thus while the *requesting services* lesson may be full of cultural information, there is unlikely to be much information of this sort to convey in other lessons—the one on *describing people* for example. The implication is clear: though it is possible to introduce cultural information in a functional design, this is not the ideal vehicle. Where this is the aim, it would be more appropriate to adopt a setting-based syllabus (containing units entitled "At the Bank", "At the Garage", "At the Post Office"), or perhaps a topic-based syllabus (containing units on "Money", "Cars", "Correspondence", "Telephones" and so on).

ii) **Number of Items on Inventory**

There may, then, be situations in which one or another of the various syllabus types immediately suggests itself as suitable for a given course with particular aims. More often than not, however, the teacher will have to apply further criteria. A second point to consider will be the extent to which the students' language needs can be usefully expressed in terms of the various item types in the syllabus inventory. Some groups of students, for example, will need to use the language in a fairly restricted number of predictable settings, and this may argue in favour of a setting-based design. A possible candidate for this type of syllabus might be a course designed to be used by doctors. It is likely that an analysis of their language needs will reveal a restricted number of settings—the consultation room, the operating theatre, the ward and so on—in which they will wish to use their English. In this case a setting-based syllabus might adequately cover the needs. But where the analysis of language needs reveals too small or too large a number of settings, this type of syllabus no longer becomes viable. Shop assistants, for example, will probably want to use the language in one setting only—the shop—and a setting-based syllabus here would suggest a one-lesson course entitled "In the Shop"! At the other extreme the students' needs may reveal a very large number of useful settings. Students living and studying at university in a foreign country, for example, will certainly need to use the language in such a variety of settings that a setting-based language course becomes an impracticable proposition.

iii) **Nature of Language**

There may thus be "mathematical" reasons influencing the choice of one or other of the various syllabus designs. A syllabus inventory which lists a few—though not too few—settings, but many functions, notions and topics, might best be covered by a setting-based syllabus; and similar arguments may be brought forward to justify any one of the other syllabus types. But mathematics alone is unlikely to provide sufficient justification. Even in a situation where it is possible to identify a manageable number of settings, for example, there may still remain persuasive arguments against a setting-based syllabus. One must also consider the way in which the language to be taught relates to the settings. There are, associated with any one setting, some language items (lexis, idiomatic expressions and even sometimes structures) whose use is more or less restricted to that setting, and perhaps one or two closely-related others. There are for example some items which are likely to be used in the restaurant setting and in very few other places. Terms like "rare", "medium" and "well done" to describe a steak are cases in point. They are "setting-specific" items of highly restricted application. But there are other language items which, though commonly used in restaurants, are not "setting-specific" in the same way. Sentences like "Will you take a cheque?" and "Could you give me a receipt?" are examples. Although these sentences are appropriate to the restaurant setting, their application is far wider, and they may be used wherever payment is required—in shops, travel agents, car-hire offices and so on.

Sometimes, especially in ESP situations, it may be the case that much of the language to be taught is of the "setting-specific" variety. In such situations a setting-based syllabus may well provide the ideal vehicle. But where the language is not so obviously setting-specific, this type of syllabus could have considerable disadvantages; non-setting-specific items will tend to repeat themselves from lesson to lesson as the various settings are covered. A syllabus which permits such repetition (unless deliberately desired for revision purposes) is not "cost effective"; that is, it does not make the most of available time. In this type of situation one should return to the syllabus inventory and ask whether another unit of organisation would be more appropriate. As noted earlier in this paper, there are many syllabus types which will cover the items on a given syllabus inventory. The criterion of cost-effectiveness demands that we should find the most economic way of doing this.

iv) Pedagogic Attractiveness

So far the criteria considered have been concerned with course aims and the nature of the items on the syllabus inventory. The students themselves are a further important variable. One often-mentioned advantage of semantic syllabuses is that they are potentially more pedagogically attractive than structural designs. It is easy to imagine that a group of students told that today they are going to learn about how to *make requests* will react with more enthusiasm than to the news that they will study the past conditional tense. How do the various semantic syllabus types distinguish themselves in terms of pedagogic attractiveness? From this point of view the setting-based syllabus (and to a large extent the topic-based syllabus also) has certain advantages over functional and notional designs. In a setting-based syllabus it is comparatively easy to link the various parts of each lesson together in a natural, vivid and concrete way. A lesson on the railway station, for example, might use a picture of a station scene as the focal point. We may ask the students to imagine and role play what various characters in the picture are saying—one at the ticket office, one at the information desk, one buying a newspaper, and so on. Settings are usually things that can be drawn, and they are certainly things that can be readily imagined. It may be similarly easy for the course writer to create concrete situations in which to practise language concerned with topics like *occupations*, *money* or *education*.

It is less easy to base a functional lesson around one concrete situation. In fact to do justice to a functional area we may be virtually obliged to introduce various unconnected situations in each lesson. To teach *greeting* adequately, for example, would entail covering a variety of situations involving different degrees of formality, different role relationships, and perhaps also in which the expected time of absence varies (cf. "See you." and "All the best."). For this reason we might say that the link between the various parts of a functional lesson tends to be a more abstract one than in the case of the setting/topic-based lesson. Similar comments may be made about notional organisation, which has the added disadvantage that some of the concepts themselves may be fairly abstract. Notions like *availability*, *temporariness* and *priority* (all in van Ek, 1975) may be difficult to convey to some students.

It is true that the extent to which materials are pedagogically attractive depends greatly on how they are written. It is possible to imagine both an exciting notional course and tedious setting-based materials. But there remain certain inherent advantages and disadvantages associated with the various syllabus types. How important a factor attractiveness is depends partly on the age and motivation of students. Though materials for all students should of course be interesting, the younger pupil will need more colour, vividness, excitement and variety than the adult. So too will the student with low motivation, and if we consider the criterion of pedagogic attractiveness alone, then there are certain advantages to setting- and topic-based designs.

v) **Student Level**

Student level is a further consideration. In the case of two semantic syllabus types—the topic- and setting-based—it is difficult to distinguish in terms of this criterion. We cannot meaningfully say that the language associated with any given *topic* is likely to be more or less difficult than the language associated with any given *setting*. A question like "Is the language used to talk about *jobs* more or less difficult than the language used in railway stations?" can find no sensible answer.[3] Thus there are no real grounds for saying that topic- and setting-based designs are distinguished in terms of difficulty and hence are more or less appropriate for any given student level. What may be said with more certainty is that there tends to be *more* language associated with given topics and settings than with given notions and functions, and one reason why topic/setting based designs are useful at the advanced level is that they permit us to introduce many varied types of language. The possibilities for exploiting a setting like the railway station are endless, and indeed it is possible to envisage quite extensive and wide-ranging language programmes based on only a handful of key settings and topics.[4] It is possible to think of functions (like *making plans*) and notions (like *past time*) which can lead to varied and wide-ranging lessons; but setting/topic-based designs tend to be looser—involving more varied language practice—and this makes them particularly suitable for the advanced level.

If we look at functional and notional designs from the same standpoint of "simplicity", there are two reasons why a notional design may be more appropriate at the lower levels. Firstly, language associated with given notions is likely to be more structurally homogeneous than language associated with given functions. Indeed, this was the reason that Wilkins referred to what are here being called notions as "semantico-*grammatical* categories", thereby reflecting the fact that they relate fairly closely to grammatical categories. The ways in which the notion of *frequency* is expressed are, in other words, more grammatically homogeneous than the ways in which functions like *inviting* or *making* arrangements are expounded.[5] If we thus accept that grammatical homogeneity is important at the lower levels, then this argues in favour of the notional as opposed to the functional syllabus at that level (always assuming that we would condone the use of any type of semantic syllabus at lower levels).[6]

Secondly, most notional teaching will tend to be at phrase, clause or sentence level, while functional teaching will often involve longer stretches of discourse. This is confirmed by a consideration of van Ek (1975). The items associated with the notion of *direction*, for example, include prepositional phrases using "to", "from", "into", "past", "across" and so on, and a teaching unit on this notion would probably wish to deal with such phrases. As the course progressed we would doubtless require the students to combine learned notions to form a variety of sentence types. If we wished to do so, and the student level demanded so, we could arrange for the notional course to contain relatively little practice above the sentence level. The items under van Ek's *apologising* on the other hand include entire sentences like "I am very sorry.", "Please forgive me." and "I do apologise." As a functional course progressed we would require the student to combine learned functions together into sometimes quite complex sequences. If we wish to do so, we could arrange for the functional course to contain a great deal of practice above the sentence level—a further reason to consider the possibility of a notional design at the lower level.

Multi-dimensionality

The criteria we have considered for the selection of one or another semantic syllabus type will rarely provide firm, black-and-white answers. Indeed (as is so often the case with criteria set up in language teaching), they will sometimes lead to conflicting conclusions. If we were to decide to use a semantic syllabus with young, fairly low level students, for example, the need for simplicity might suggest a notional design while the need for pedagogic attractiveness would argue in favour of a setting/topic-based organisation. In such cases the language teacher must do what over time he has had much practice in doing—weigh relative advantages and disadvantages to reach some compromise.

In one important sense, though, the syllabus designer's task is easier than has so far been suggested. This is because we have assumed he has an exclusive choice—he must choose functional *or* notional *or* setting-based *or* topic-based design. This assumption has been made in order to examine in as clear a way as possible the implications involved in adopting the various syllabus types. But it is a false assumption and there is no reason why only *one* of the inventory item types need be selected as the unit of organisation. It would be possible to develop a syllabus leading to lessons of varying orientation—some covering important functions, others dealing with settings and topics, and yet others perhaps with notions or structures. Once we begin to think in terms of a syllabus which is *multi-dimensional* rather than *uni-dimensional*, many of the conflicting conclusions from the criteria discussed above will disappear, and the result will be a syllabus design which is less rigid and more sensitive to the various student language needs.

The following example illustrates both how some of the criteria discussed above can be applied, and also the kind of reasons which may lead the course designer to think in terms of a multi-dimensional syllabus. In 1974 the Centre for Applied Language Studies at the University of Reading set about preparing spoken English materials for use on a presessional language course.[7] This course was for overseas students about to begin programmes of postgraduate study at British universities, and the aim of the spoken English materials was to meet some of their social needs. After applying the type of criteria considered above it was decided that the best overall design for the materials would be a functional one.

But although a functional design was found to meet most of the required aims, there were some that it did not meet so well. One objective was to give the students—more or less as soon as the course began—language relevant to their immediate needs on coming to live in Britain—a type of survival kit to help them through the first few weeks of their stay. Some of this language could be adequately handled by functional units. For example, the students would need to perform—more or less on arrival—such basic communicative acts as *greeting*, *introducing themselves*, *saying goodbye*. These immediately useful functions were placed at the beginning of the syllabus, and were referred to as "Preliminary functional units" to distinguish them from the "Main functional units" that followed.

But other of the students' immediate language needs were closely associated with a small number of settings and topics. For example, they would need to learn as early as possible how to open a bank account, make overseas telephone calls, register with the police and doctor, and these needs could best be met by setting/topic-based units. Eight immediately useful topics and settings were isolated and the units dealing with these were placed after the "Preliminary functional units". At this point the course design looked like this:

1. Preliminary functional units
2. Setting/topic units
3. Main functional units

No sooner had this design been arrived at, however, than it was found to need modification. This was because although much of the language associated with the chosen settings and topics was what was earlier called "setting/topic-specific" (items like "current account", "cheque book", "overdraft" associated with the bank setting for example), this was not true of all items. There were certain functions which occurred so frequently in the chosen settings and topics, that cost-effectiveness required them to be taught separately. Items like "I'd like to . . . ." and "Could you please . . .?" are useful in opening a bank account, making an overseas phone call, registering with the police and doctor. Far more sensible to treat these items once and for all in a single unit dealing with *requesting services* than to deal with them separately each time they occurred in the setting/topic units. Apart from *requesting services* there were several other functions of this sort, and the obvious place to treat these was in a short series of units placed before the setting/topic units. The syllabus design was therefore modified:

1. Preliminary functional units
2. Units covering functions recurring in the setting/topic units
3. Setting/topic units
4. Main functional units

This example of a multi-dimensional syllabus contains units of three different orientations: functional, setting and topic. In other situations the materials designer will wish to introduce other combinations. He may, for example, follow a series of functional units by one or two structural lessons which deal in a systematic way with important structures, introduced in the functional units but not there given the amount of attention they require.[8] Indeed this flexibility to change the focal point of the teaching materials as the course unfolds can be regarded as one of the major advances in syllabus design which the semantic approach provides. One must of course be careful not to change the orientation of the materials too often, as this is likely to confuse the students. But the freedom to shift orientation takes one far from the days of the traditional structural syllabus which results in lessons confining themselves largely to one dimension of language behaviour—structural correctness.[9]

Notes

1. The terms "semantic syllabus inventory" and "semantic syllabus" are used throughout this book to refer to inventories and syllabuses drawn up in notional/functional terms. For the justification of this usage, see page 39.
2. This point is taken up in Paper 8 in relation to the teaching of beginners.
3. The same point is made in relation to distinguishing functions, in Paper 5.
4. The materials discussed in Paper 7 are a case in point.
5. This point is amplified in Paper 3.
6. Paper 8 argues against the use of semantic syllabuses with beginners.
7. These materials were subsequently rewritten for a more general audience, and appeared as Morrow and Johnson (1979). The initial course design described here was drawn up by D. A. Wilkins, K. Morrow and me. The materials are discussed further in Paper 5.
8. The draft materials here described did in fact also contain a "grammatical follow up" which provided structural practice for those students needing it. The final version of the materials (Morrow and Johnson, 1979) contains "consolidation units" which systematically deal with structures in the way described here.
9. Another example of multi-dimensionality is given in Paper 7.

Paper 5:

Unit Ordering and Handling Different Proficiency Levels

The first part of this paper deals with another problem related to the conversion of syllabus inventory into syllabus—that of unit ordering. In the structural syllabus one of the main criteria for this was structural simplicity; units covering simpler structures were placed before those covering more complex structures. In a semantic syllabus a simplicity criterion is less easy to apply, and the paper considers possible alternative criteria. The second part of the paper looks at ways in which one set of teaching materials can be devised to handle different student levels. This will be particularly relevant to those teaching in situations where a variety of levels must be taught, but where resources for materials production are limited.

This paper is a revised version of one delivered at a SELMOUS seminar on "Pre-sessional English courses for overseas students in higher education" held at Manchester in April 1977. The proceedings of this seminar appear as ELT Documents, ETIC (1978).

IN 1974, the Centre for Applied Language Studies at the University of Reading began preparing a set of Social English materials for use on its pre-sessional summer course.[1] The aims of this paper are to describe the rationale behind parts of their original design and to discuss ways in which the materials, after several years of use, have withstood the test of time.

Unit Ordering

The question of unit ordering is an important one whatever the syllabus design. When the design is grammatical, it is usual to apply a structural simplicity criterion to determine which items should be taught earlier, which later. Although there are of course problems associated with all simplicity criteria, the procedure does at least ensure that a unit ordering is arrived at in a principled way. When the design is semantic on the other hand, a structural simplicity criterion cannot be so easily applied. It is generally true that the language associated with any one function is structurally as simple or complex as the language associated with any other function. It may be the case that there is more language which one would want to teach in association with one function (such as *describing people*) than with another (such as *greeting*). To this extent—the extent that "more" entails "more complex"—it is possible to arrive at an ordering of some functions in terms of "simplicity". But it is an easy matter to find examples of *greetings* which, by any simplicity criterion, are more complex than chosen *descriptions of people*. (a) and (b) illustrate this:

> a. Why hallo, George. I haven't seen you in weeks. How's the wife keeping? I heard she'd been ill.
> b. He's very tall.

A simplicity criterion is, then, of restricted value. A second possible criterion considers "priority of needs". It is certainly possible to identify some activities—such as opening a bank account, registering with the doctor (and with these, associated functions like *giving personal information, requesting services*)—which the student will need to learn about early in his stay. Many of these early requirements are associated with a fixed number of topics and settings, and it is for this reason that the topic/setting-based units appear early in the course.

Again, however, the criterion has restrictions. It cannot be applied to all the functions one wishes to teach, and questions like "Do the students need to learn how to *apologise* before learning how to *interrupt?*" have no clear answer.

Also, the findings which the application of this criterion provide cannot be easily translated into syllabus design terms. The findings are that there are two types of function (setting and topic)—those which the student needs to know about very early on in his stay, and those to which no priority of need at all can be attached. Unfortunately the functions which need to be taught very early on are likely to be so numerous as to make anything but a token application of this criterion meaningless. One soon finds oneself having to make decisions like whether regis-tration with a doctor is more urgent than opening a bank account. Will the students be ill before they need money? Or vice versa?

The initial course design certainly placed more faith in this criterion than has turned out to be justified, and experience has suggested that any systematic attempt to grade semantic items according to priority of need can only succeed to a restricted extent.

"Sequencing potential" was another criterion much used in the course design.[2] A syllabus may be said to have high sequencing potential if it provides the students with plenty of opportunities for sequencing the taught functions together to form longer interactions. If, for example, the functions *greet, invite, make arrangements* are taught in consecutive units, it becomes an easy matter to provide role play exercises in which the student greets a friend, invites him to dinner, makes arrangements about where and when to meet. If these functions are not treated consecutively (but, say, in units 3, 9, 15) then a role play exercise of this type cannot be given until the last of the three units (unit 15) has been taught. A syllabus constructed without concern for sequencing potential will miss many opportunities to give regular practice in sustained conversational interchanges.[3]

However useful this criterion might be, there are again restrictions on its application. Many functions fall naturally within sequences involving more than one participant, each of whose behaviour is reasonably predictable. Examples might be *inviting* and *greeting*. It is a viable generalisation to say that an inviting move is generally followed by an accepting or declining move. Acceptance may in turn be followed by a sequence in which arrangements are made. Similarly a greeting will often be followed by a returned greeting and perhaps by an invitation ("Come in and have a drink."), an expression of solicitude ("How's Jane? I hear she's been ill."), or the like. In teaching what might be termed "interactive" functions of this sort, there are positive advantages in presenting them within the sort of sequences in which they occur, and the criterion of "sequencing potential" may therefore be applied. But other functions are not interactive in the same way. Some, like *describing people* or *expressing feelings* characteristically involve one person only, and it is therefore difficult (and unnecessary) to link the units dealing with these functions to preceding or subsequent ones. In other cases the participation of the interactant is quite unpredictable. For example, although the function of *interrupting* must by its nature occur as part of a sequence involving at least two people, the participation of the "interuptee" is not sufficiently predictable for a sequence of moves involving both participants to be made the basis for unit ordering.

Providing Materials for Various Proficiency Levels

Most pre-sessional courses face the problem of providing materials for a large variety of proficiency levels. The Reading pre-sessional has at its peak as many as twenty classes graded (for some activities at least) by performance on an initial proficiency test.

When Social English materials were first produced it was assumed that most students, however grammatically sophisticated they might be, would to a large extent be communicatively "naive". Their systemic knowledge[4] might be excellent; but this does not necessarily imply a knowledge of how to *greet, invite, make arrangements* in socially acceptable ways. This would, it was predicted, hold true particularly for "situationally-bound" language. Most students would not for example know lexical items like "budget account", "overdrawn", "to cross a cheque", essential to functioning in the bank setting.

For this reason it was decided not to level the materials in Book I, which contains the situationally-bound language of the setting-/topic-based units.[5] The experience of the 1974 pre-sessional course served to indicate that this decision was justified, but by 1976 a gradual change in the student population had become apparent. More students from oil-rich countries attended the course. Because of their financial position many had already spent time in England, and some indeed had travelled widely through Britain and Europe. Consequently when the course began they already possessed some of the basic communicative knowledge Book I was designed to teach. The implication is that some means of grading is necessary even for this book.

A number of criteria were used to level the materials in Book II. Again an attempt was made to use a syntactic simplicity criterion. Again problems were encountered. Is "How about coming to the theatre?" a more complex or simple exponent of *inviting* than "Why not come to the theatre?" The difficulties of using this criterion meaningfully are compounded by the fact that with multi-lingual groups simplicity cannot be determined on contrastive grounds.[6]

A more useful criterion is that of utterance length, expressed in terms similar to those used by Sinclair and Coulthard (1975), (a), (b) and (c), for example, represent three exponents of *inviting* suitable for teaching at three levels. They differ in terms of length:

a. Would you like to come to our party on Saturday?
b. It's our wedding anniversary on Saturday and we're having a party. Would you like to come?
c. It's our wedding anniversary on Saturday and we're having a party. Would you like to come? We haven't seen you for ages.

(a) is a simple invitation. In (b) there is a "pre-head" in which the speaker states what the occasion for celebration is. The invitation in (c) is followed by a "post-head" in which the speaker gives an extra reason for the invitation.

A third criterion involves the notion of "transparency".[7] (a), (b) and (c) illustrate three utterances which might, under certain conditions, be interpreted as requests (for someone to open a window):

a. Would you mind opening the window?
b. I wish someone would open the window.
c. It's really stuffy in here.

Of course, (a) is most "transparently" a request. It uses a form ("Would you mind . . . ?") frequently associated with requests in English. (b) is less transparently so. On the surface it is merely the expression of a wish, and only in certain circumstances would the listener be led to interpret it as a request. (c) is the most "opaque" of the three. Here the speaker appears merely to be stating a fact. Again, in certain situations this utterance might be interpreted as a request.

There may be an argument for introducing the most opaque exponents of a function at a higher level. It is partly a question of "generativity". The more transparent exponents can usually be used in a large variety of situations, just as in the example considered "Would you mind . . .?" can be used to "generate" a large number of requests. For this reason there are advantages in introducing transparent exponents to all students. Learning to request by expressing a wish or stating a fact is in a sense a secondary issue which can be left to the higher level.

One criterion which has not received much theoretical attention in the past is grading by exercise type. It is uncontroversially the case that the higher the student level and the better he is able to manipulate the language, the more communicatively complex the tasks he can undertake. While the lower level student might only with difficulty be able to do a simple drill, the advanced student will be able to process quite complex pieces of information and respond to them in a variety of ways. The notion of communicative complexity is as yet a relatively unexplored one, but there are obvious ways in which what may be expected of a student in a communicative situation may be made more simple or complex. We may vary the amount of choice he is given as to what to say; how much advance information he is given as to what the interaction to be practised is about (and how his interactant will respond); we may vary the degree of importance we place on rapid response, on the ability to predict what is about to be said, on the degree of redundancy necessary for comprehension. Such measures of communicative skill have so far largely been ignored in communicative language teaching.

This criterion of complexity of communicative task is used in parts of the Social English Materials. These materials are experimental, and part of the experiment is to utilise various patterns of unit organisation in order to identify the most suitable. One pattern is illustrated overleaf.

The principle is that the students should do as much of each unit as possible in the allotted time. The minimum is the common core, and there is no information contained in the other modules which is essential to the student in subsequent units. A student who only covers the common core can therefore proceed to the next unit without difficulties. Intermediate students pass from the common core into the diagnostic

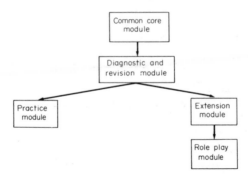

and revision module. This module consists of a series of short role plays, designed to reveal to the teacher particular areas of difficulty which the students may be encountering. If it is clear that the students need further practice in the language introduced in the common core, they then pass on to the practice module. If not they proceed to the extension module which introduces new items and includes more complex exercise types. The advanced student will then have time to move to the role play module. The tasks set in this are fairly complex and the students are given considerable freedom as to how to fulful their respective roles.

No study has yet been done on the effectiveness of the various patterns of unit organisation introduced. But the pattern described above certainly goes a long way to provide the degree of flexibility required for the pre-sessional situation in which variety of levels is a major problem.

Notes

1. For more details of these materials and of the pre-sessional course, see page 67 and Note 7 on page 69.
2. For further discussion of this criterion, see Paper 6 and Paper 13.
3. Since it is one of the aims of discourse analysis of the Sinclair and Coulthard (1975) type (discussed in Paper 1 of this volume) to identify characteristic sequences of functions, such studies will eventually provide the materials designer with much useful information in this area.
4. For the way in which this term is being used, see page 9 and Note 3 on page 22.
5. For more details on these units and on the course design in general, see Paper 4.
6. For detailed discussion of the kind of problems a simplicity criterion introduces, see Paper 7.
7. This concept has been discussed in relation to testing in Morrow (1977).

Paper 6:

Semantic Syllabus Design for Written English

Though this paper considers practical questions of syllabus design, its tone is theoretical. Its immediate concern is with the teaching of academic writing, but the issues it discusses are relevant to all areas of syllabus design. Anyone who has attempted to design a semantic syllabus will have found himself faced with a plethora of functional and notional labels, and will probably have searched for some kind of coherent framework within which to organise these. The paper describes one attempt to overcome such problems. It was delivered at the Annual General Meeting of the British Association for Applied Linguistics, September, 1976.

THE WORK which provided the stimulus for this discussion was the preparation of an academic writing course to be used as part of a pre-sessional programme organised by the Centre for Applied Language Studies at the University of Reading. The aim of this paper is primarily descriptive: to present the rationale behind the approach taken for this course, focusing attention on problems of general interest to those concerned with writing course design.[1]

Possible Frameworks

The initial strategy adopted as a prelude to course design was to attempt to characterise specimens of appropriate texts in functional terms—appropriate texts in this case being examples of descriptive and argumentative prose taken from the large variety of disciplines which the course participants would eventually be studying. Such analyses would, it was hoped, identify the most frequently occurring functions, which the course would then teach. It would also indicate ways in which these functions are characteristically sequenced to produce coherent discourse.

It soon became clear, however, that such a strategy could not succeed without reference to a theoretical framework. In the absence of such a framework a plethora of labels may be applied, in a quite arbitrary and unrevealing way, to describe the function of any given element of discourse. Something like Sinclair and Coulthard's (1975) analysis of classroom discourse, but directed to academic prose, would be required if the texts were to be approached in a principled way. Unfortunately time did not permit nearly so elaborate an analysis, and the approach adopted was thus inevitably makeshift. The following remarks are observations on what a framework can be expected to provide, and how it might be developed.

One obvious theoretical requirement is the specification of a set of ranks at which the analysis would operate. The need for such a specification in functional analyses has been noted by others (for example in Candlin, 1976) and will not be discussed here, except to observe that the functional inventories already in existence do not seem to have been drawn up with any one rank consistently in mind. The categories found in van Ek's *The Threshold Level* (1975) for example, appear to associate themselves with elements of discourse varying very considerably in size—a fact which in our experience at the Centre severely restricts the pedagogic utility of that document as the basis for general course design.[2] In the specific area of formal written English attempts have been made to define certain units of discourse, examples being Lackstrom, Selinker and Trimble's (1973) "conceptual paragraphs" and Kaplan's (1975) "discourse blocks". But so far the approaches have been piecemeal and such units do not take their place within fully worked-out models.

A theoretical framework would also specify the parameters along which functional analysis would proceed. Others, again, have noted the need for this, and despite the existence of theoretical models such as

Halliday's with his parameters of "ideational", "textual" and "interpersonal", it is only now that attempts are being made to develop models specifically for pedagogic purposes.[3] Consequently the taxonomies so far used for course design appear confused in this respect and, as Candlin (1976) points out, often contain categories which characterise the elements of discourse in quite different ways.

Despite this confusion, a consideration of the course designs currently available does reveal two distinct parameters used in the analysis of written discourse. The first involves categories of the type found in Wilkins (1973) and referred to as categories of "communicative functions". These categories relate the elements to the communicative operations they perform, and provide labels such as "definition", "classification", "cause and effect", etc. The second parameter is particularly (though not exclusively, since elements of this approach are found in Sinclair and Coulthard, 1975, and others) associated with the rhetorical systems of American writers such as Kaplan, Pitkin and Christensen. Characteristic of their approach is the analysis of texts predominantly in terms of how the utterances relate to each other within the framework of the discourse. Hence an element will be described as an "introducer", a "modifier", a "developer", an "intensifier", a "particularisation", a "supporting statement", etc. Such labels might be said to characterise the element's "rhetorical function".

These two parameters, the communicative and rhetorical, have been variously used as the basis for course design. Some writers, such as Cowie and Heaton (in experimental materials reported in Cowie and Heaton, 1975) confine themselves to communicative functions. These may be arranged in arbitrary order, or grouped according to some other principle—Jones and Faulkner (1971), for example, categorise functions according to the type of logical operation they are said to entail. Similar to this procedure in general course design would be to present functions grouped under the superordinate headings found in Wilkins (1973). This would result in blocks of units concerned with "moral discipline and education", "suasion", "emotional relations" and the like.

Other textbooks, particularly those used to teach composition writing to freshmen of American universities (for example, Buckler and Sklare, 1966; Pichaske, 1975) concentrate attention on rhetorical functions. Such books take either the paragraph or the essay as their primary unit, and deal with various rhetorical types—expository, argumentative, narrative, descriptive, etc. These are characteristically further categorised for each type in terms of discourse positions—i.e. introductions, developments and conclusions.

Though for the purposes of exposition it may be useful to characterise existing textbooks as being either "communicative" or "rhetorical" in orientation, it is in fact quite rare to find examples which are exclusively the one or the other. More commonly, writing coursebooks either ignore the distinction or do not observe it consistently, utilising categories of both types in arbitrary sequence. But clearly the possibility for a third course design does exist: one in which a systematic attempt is made to cover both communicative and rhetorical functions. Such an approach would first entail an analysis of texts specifying both the rhetorical and communicative functions of the constituent elements. As the next step in the production of a course design, one would then generalise over a large number of texts to identify which communicative functions characteristically operate within which discourse positions. We might for example find that "definitions" and "classifications" occur most commonly in the introductions to pieces of expository prose, while "contrasts" and "comparisons" on the other hand are associated with developmental paragraphs. The feasibility of such a procedure would of course depend on the extent to which meaningful generalisations of this kind can be made—an issue to which we return in the last section of this paper. An approach somewhat akin to the one being described here, though not directed towards written English, is outlined in Riley (1976) who speaks of "communicative" and "discursive" levels of analysis. For written English, Imhoof and Hudson's course design (1975) appears to move in the same direction.

A theoretical framework would, then, specify not only a set of ranks, but also the parameters in terms of which the analysis underlying course design would operate. Considering two such parameters—the communicative and the rhetorical—at least three approaches (we have seen) are possible and have to varying degrees of consistency been followed. The first concentrates attention on communicative functions only; the second on rhetorical functions only, while the third—based on an analysis of texts specifying the communicative and rhetorical functions of constituent elements—utilises both parameters.

Selecting the Framework for a
Pre-Sessional Writing Course

Passing now to matters more directly concerned with pedagogy, it is clear that which of these three approaches is appropriate will depend on the specific aims of the course under consideration. In the case of the pre-sessional writing programme two aims are felt to be particularly important. The first is to ensure that the student can recognise and produce exponents associated with the communicative functions most commonly found in academic writing; the second is to offer him practice in sequencing these functions to produce coherent discourse. Thus an appropriate course design would not only permit introduction of the relevant communicative functions; it would also have what might be called "sequencing potential"—that is, the means for readily providing practice in linking the taught functions together to form larger discourse units.[4]

It is only really the third of the approaches described above which can adequately meet both these aims. A course design specified in communicative terms alone meets the aim of introducing and practising communicative functions. But this type of organisation, if adopted exclusively, has little "sequencing potential". With each teaching unit either totally unrelated to the next, or related only in some "abstract" way, providing practice in chaining functions together becomes difficult (though not, of course, impossible). The teaching units are arranged according to principles other than their potential to generate characteristic sequences, and hence the organisation itself does not facilitate this process.

The second type of course design, which focuses attention on rhetorical function, has on the other hand great sequencing potential. Hence its use in L_1 rhetorical handbooks whose main purpose is to concentrate on coherence. But such handbooks are for students who supposedly already know how to expound the various communicative functions, an assumption which cannot be made for foreign students. By de-emphasising the importance of communicative function, this type of design fails to meet one aim of the pre-sessional writing programme.

One way in which the third approach might meet these aims would simply be by grouping communicative functions in the first instance according to the discourse positions, in ways which the prior analysis of texts would have identified as being characteristic. This might produce an organisation in three parts, dealing with "introductions", "developments" and "conclusions". With each teaching unit covering one communicative function, such an organisation would provide an adequate vehicle for introducing and practising each in isolation; but it would also have sequencing potential: once all the functions associated with "introductions", for example, have been taught, these may be practised linked together in characteristic permutations to form introductions to various types of discourse.

In this way the third approach is suited to the requirements of the pre-sessional writing course. But there is another criterion to be considered, according to which this design is less satisfactory. It is the criterion of what Wilkins (1974) has called "high surrender value". A course is said to have "high surrender value" if the effort the student invests in learning is quickly rewarded by high returns in ability to communicate.[5] One way in which this may be achieved is by careful selection of the items to be taught. Hence a general justification of the semantic syllabus, as opposed to the conventional grammatical one, is that it yields only those areas of language use identified as being relevant to the students' language needs—rather than attempting to teach the entire language system. In this way it yields a quick return on time invested.

But there is a way in which a course may achieve what might be called "high *internal* surrender value". This is by judicious arrangement of materials within the course, to ensure that from an early point the student receives regular returns on his investment. If he has to wait until the end of the course before reaping the benefits of his effort, the design may be said to have low internal surrender value. A criticism sometimes levelled at the structural syllabus is that only when the programme is completed does the student have the linguistic tools at his disposal to use the language as he wishes. But this criticism may equally apply to a functionally organised syllabus. Hence in the first approach discussed in this paper, where communicative functions are arranged arbitrarily or according to some abstract principle, it is not until the end of the course that the student possesses the tool to produce the paragraphs and essays he wishes to write. With the functions arranged according to discourse positions—the third approach considered—the student is soon able to produce introductory, developmental and concluding paragraphs. But it is not until the end of the course that entire essays can be written, and to this extent the same criticism applies. Thus while these two syllabus designs may, through careful selection of the items to be taught, gain high *external* surrender value—in relation, that is, to designs for other courses of similar duration—their *internal* surrender value remains low.

The type of organisation which would yield high internal surrender value would be one in which the design is made up of self-contained sets of units, each dealing with one discrete area of the required terminal behaviour. An alternative to the "discourse position" approach, and in fact the one used as the basis for the pre-sessional writing course, achieves this by making an initial categorisation in terms of rhetorical type and topic. Table 1 illustrates the procedure undertaken.

Relevant areas of discourse were analysed in the first place in terms of rhetorical type, the two main areas being descriptive or expository, and

TABLE 1

Discourse type	Discourse type	Discourse position	Example functions
Exposition	Describing phenomena and ideas	Introduction	Defining, Classifying, Identifying
		Development	Contrasting, Exemplifying
		Conclusion	Summary
	Describing processes	Introduction	Describing purpose, Describing means
		Development	Sequential description, Instructions
		Conclusion	Summary, Describing results
Argumentation	Argumentation	Introduction	Stating a proposition, Stating assumptions
		Development	Induction, Deduction, Substantiation, Concession
		Conclusion	Summary, Generalisation, Speculation

argumentation. The second categorisation is a subdivision of description according to discourse topic, yielding "describing phenomena and ideas" on the one hand and "describing processes" (the "process analyses" of the rhetorical handbook) on the other. Further subcategorisation then proceeds according to discourse position (i.e. introduction, development, conclusion). The materials therefore contain three self-contained sets of units, dealing with "describing phenomena and ideas", "describing processes" and "argumentation". As soon as the first has been covered (approximately a third of the way through the course), the student is in a position to produce essays of the relevant rhetorical type. In this way the design has high internal surrender value.

It is worth noting that apart from any general pedagogic justification for creating a course with high internal surrender value, there is a particular—and rather mundane—reason why the criterion is important for the pre-sessional writing course. It is that some of the students cannot attend the course for its duration. Working on the assumption that it is better to teach such students one small thing completely, rather than half a larger thing, a design made up of self-contained sets of units has distinct advantages.

In this section a number of criteria for the evaluation of writing course designs have been mentioned, and particular attention has been paid to two (related) criteria: sequencing potential and internal surrender value. These provide some justification for the approach outlined in Table 1.

Assumptions Behind the Approach

The validity of the proposed approach is based on two assumptions, both of which are open to challenge. The first is that the introductions, developments and conclusions to essays of each rhetorical type are sufficiently dissimilar to warrant separate treatment. The analysis of academic prose undertaken as a prelude to course design suggests that this is indeed the case. However, there are (not surprisingly) certain areas where the functions associated with a discourse position are the same for each rhetorical type. It was found, for example, that the concluding devices used for descriptions, process analyses and argumentation were often the same. In this situation a criterion of cost effectiveness, which would require concluding devices to be treated together in a block, conflicts with the criterion of high internal surrender value whereby such devices would be introduced at appropriate points throughout the course, thus making it possible for the students to write entire essays. In this particular case, and for the purposes of the draft edition, cost effectiveness was considered to be the more important criterion, and the concluding devices are introduced together in a block. The final course design, which includes a number of orientation units intended to introduce the student to the approach of the course, is given as the Appendix to this paper.

The second assumption concerns a fundamental question which has already been raised (for example, in Candlin, 1976) with relation to functional materials in general. It is to what extent norms can be prescribed. The aspect of this question most relevant here is the extent to which communicative functions can meaningfully be associated with certain discourse positions. In the model illustrated in Table 1, "definitions" (for example) are included under "introductions to descriptions of phenomena and ideas", a designation that may lead the student to believe either that such introductions must necessarily contain a definition, or that definitions cannot be found in other discourse positions connected with other rhetorical types—both statements being patently untrue.

The validity of the approach rests, then, on the assumption that characteristic sequences of communicative functions can be identified for specific rhetorical types and discourse positions. Such analysis of text as was undertaken in fact supports this assumption, as long as the word "characteristic" is well stressed. This gives the approach an (admittedly small) degree of linguistic justification which, one might predict, the development of studies of the sort initiated by Kaplan on comparative rhetorical structures is likely eventually to reinforce. But by far the most important justification is pedagogic. The communicative functions are arranged as they are mainly to provide a vehicle for the generation of longer stretches of discourse. Hence "definitions", "classifications", and what have been called "identifications" are included under "introducing descriptions of phenomena and ideas" simply because of their sequencing potential in that position. Any implication (at this early experimental stage) that the sequences thus generated have prescriptive value is to be eschewed.

An attempt to counteract the dangers of prescription has been made along two fronts. The first involves the so-called "consolidation units", appearing in boxes in the Appendix. Most of these units bear labels referring to discourse type and position, and one of their aims is to provide sequencing practice. Thus, once the functions associated with "developing an argument" have been dealt with discretely in Units 23–5, Unit 26 practises them chained together in various permutations. But an equally important aim of these consolidation units is to introduce functions other than those explictly taught in the course, in a variety of permutations. In this way the student is exposed to functional sequences other than those which he has previously practised intensively.

The second means is concerned with the total structure of the pre-sessional writing programme of which the materials under discussion are only a part. It is a fundamental necessity of all syllabuses of the type which Wilkins (1976) has termed "synthetic"—and the syllabus described here is of this sort—that they should be counterbalanced by considerable exposure to authentic texts which do not necessarily follow the norms selected for "synthetic" teaching.[6] For this reason the present writing course is eventually to be linked to the pre-sessional reading programme. Both will have a similar organisation. Thus the reading programme will, for example, begin with descriptive and move on to argumentation texts. Each text studied will naturally provide examples of various communicative functions (only some of which will be covered in the writing course) sequenced in various ways. Follow-up exercises will draw attention to these various sequences and will make an explicit link between the writing and reading programmes.

The course design, therefore, does not imply any prescriptive status for the sequences it hopes to generate: and any impression of prescription that the course may give is counteracted in the consolidation units and through links with other areas of the pre-sessional programme.

Appendix[7]

A. Introductory units	Number of units
1. Functions, and types of discourse	1
2. Topic and comment/old and new information	1
3. Degrees of categoriality/the status and value of propositions	1
4. Cause and effect	
5. Reason, result consequence	1
B. Characterising phenomena and ideas	
6. Defining	2
7. Classifying	2
8. Identifying	1
9. Characterising phenomena and ideas	1
C. Describing phenomena and ideas	
10. Contrasting and comparing	2
11. Exemplifying	2
12. Particularising, generalising, intensifying	1
13. Types of description statement	1
14. Structuring a description	1
D. Introducing a process analysis	
15. Purpose and means	1
16. Prediction and expectancy	1
17. Introducing a process analysis	1

Number of units

E. Developing a process analysis

    18. Sequential description   2

    19. Issuing instructions   1

    | 20. Describing a process analysis | 1

F. 21. [linking unit: Description and argumentation]   1

G. Argumentation

    | 22. Introducing an argument | 1

    23. Substantiation   2

    24. Modification   2

    25. Implication   2

    | 26. Development an argument | 1

H. Concluding

    27. Summarising   2

    28. Drawing conclusions   2

    29. Expressing personal view/assessment   1

    | 30. Concluding a description or argument | 1

Total   40

40 units of one hour's duration

Notes

1. The materials have been rewritten for a wider audience and appear in a substantially changed form as Johnson (1981). Paper 19 discusses the reasons for these changes.
2. This shortcoming is further discussed in Paper 7.
3. See Halliday (1970b) for details of his three parameters.
4. See Paper 5 for further discussion of "sequencing potential".
5. The concept of surrender value is also discussed in Papers 8 and 9.
6. The concept of "synthetic" is considered at greater length in Paper 10.
7. Considerable changes were made to this design in the final version (Johnson, 1981), mainly to make the course shorter.

Paper 7:

The Adoption of Functional Syllabuses for General Language Teaching Courses

The previous papers in Section 2 have dealt with practical problems of syllabus design. This paper and the following two are more concerned with questions of application, and consider the relevance of semantic syllabuses to various teaching situations. Paper 7 concentrates on "general courses". But despite this shift in emphasis, the paper is linked to earlier ones because it reintroduces, within the context of one concrete teaching situation, a number of problems discussed earlier. Also, because of the number of doubts which this paper expresses (again in relation to one concrete teaching situation) it looks forward to Section 3 where similar doubts are discussed in more theoretical terms.

This paper was published in the Canadian Modern Language Review, **33**, 5, 1977. *It is a revised version of one which first appeared in* ELT Documents, **76**, **1**, 1976. *It was first written in 1976, hence the reference on the first page to over two years having passed since Wilkins' 1973 paper.*

Part 1 of this paper contains observations concerning the suitability of functional syllabuses as a basis for general course design. Part 2 considers how functionally orientated materials may be integrated within existing language teaching programmes.[1]

Part 1

IT IS now over two years since the original proposals for functional syllabus design were made available in accessible form (Wilkins, 1973).

Since that time the ideas have received widespread attention, to the extent that today course designers, examining boards and others whose decisions are likely to affect language teaching programmes in crucial ways are already considering adoption of such syllabus designs, while materials claiming to be functional in orientation are beginning to appear. The idea has, in short, "caught on".

As with many ideas that achieve relatively sudden popularity in this way, there is the danger that more will be claimed for these syllabuses than was originally intended. The danger has not passed unmarked. Wilkins (1974), for example, emphasises that though such syllabuses may provide satisfactory frameworks for certain types of course, their suitability for "general courses" (e.g. long duration school courses designed to cater for a variety of often only vaguely specifiable language needs) is as yet in doubt.[2] As for the suggestion that in the present state of the art functional syllabuses should replace grammatical ones, this is seen as being "decidedly premature" (Wilkins, 1974, p. 120). The continuing flurry of interest suggests that such warnings may go unheeded. The danger grows that syllabuses developed in many parts of the world and sometimes affecting the future language teaching strategies of entire nations, may change all too prematurely; that (as an inevitable consequence) functional materials should appear on the market with a rapidity indicating that they can differ from previous structurally-based materials in only the most superficial of ways.

Given such a situation it seems appropriate to reiterate, and elaborate on, some previously given warnings. Underlying everything to be said is the conviction that there is indeed a place for functional materials in general course design, despite the considerable problems that production of these materials is likely to pose. By dwelling on areas of difficulty and unclear application the intention is simply to strike a note of caution for syllabus designers and course writers who may be contemplating adoption of a functional framework.

Functions, Grammar and Levels

To recognise the desirability of a functional approach is not in any way to claim that structural knowledge of the language is unnecessary or unimportant. Grammatical competence is a part of communicative competence, and the language teacher is clearly committed to ensuring that his students are able to manipulate the language structurally (entailing "grammatical knowledge") as well as use it appropriately (entailing "functional knowledge"). Given such a commitment, it is relevant to ask to what extent the functional syllabus may provide a suitable framework for tackling the former task.

In functional language teaching materials the items to be taught are grouped (as already noted) according to ways in which they may be used, to form units bearing such titles as "Greetings", "Making Requests", "Invitations", etc. We may wish our unit on "Making Requests", for example, to introduce exponents such as "Would you mind opening the window?", "Could you open the window, please?" and "Open the window, please." Though these sentences may function in a similar way, they are structurally quite dissimilar, and indeed it seems reasonable to expect sentences which form a homogeneous functional grouping to be grammatically unlike (cf. Widdowson, 1971). The choice of a functional organisation therefore seems to imply a degree of structural "disorganisation", to the extent that many structurally dissimilar sentences may be presented in the same unit, while what may be taken to be key examples of particular grammatical structures will be scattered throughout the course.

Indeed, it is difficult to impose any kind of structural grading on a functional syllabus. It does not seem to be generally the case that the language used to expound one function is structurally any simpler or more complex than the language used to expound any other. The "language of greeting" may be as simple or as complex as the "language of inviting", for example. Hence it is (generally, and with some specific exceptions) impossible to ensure structural progression simply by ordering the units in a particular way. We may be tempted to impose an artificial structural grading (as at times doubtless cannot be avoided), ensuring that grammatically complex structures are made to follow structurally simple ones by careful selection of the exponents to be introduced. If the materials are to remain functionally accurate the degree to which this may legitimately be done is clearly restricted; and anyway the resulting structural progression will in no way approach the carefully plotted grammatical grading found in a well designed structural syllabus.

The course writer who attempts to reconcile functional organisation with structural grading is thus constantly faced with problems of this type: he wishes to introduce the ("complex") structure "Would you mind opening the window?" in the unit of "Making Requests"; indeed, he feels that to omit such a common form of requesting from the unit would be to commit a functional travesty. Yet this unit may occur early in the course, before other units containing structurally related but "simpler" sentences such as "I would like to open the window." (with the "would" form) and "I'm opening the window." (with the "-ing" form). An alternative to functional travesty is to switch unit order, so as to ensure that the "simpler" sentences are introduced before the more complex one; but this will certainly create other equally serious structural anomalies, since every unit introduces a number of exponents of varied structural complexity.

Structural practice within a functional design is of course possible. After the introduction of "I haven't seen you for three weeks." in a unit on "Greetings" for example, one strategy would involve the teacher interrupting the (functional) flow of the lesson to provide a grammatical explanation—a difficult and lengthy task, however, unless students are already familiar with the present perfect and time constructions using "for". A structural drill may even be given, though if the functional organisation is to be maintained, one might wish to argue that examples which are not associated with greeting (but which may nevertheless be grammatically crucial examples) will have to be excluded. Given that the sentence under consideration is almost certainly but one of a number of structurally heterogeneous exponents introduced in the "Greetings" unit, the teacher will also be forced by time constraints into a selection of grammar points for detailed treatment which will most likely exclude many sentences deserving equally thorough consideration. Add to this the fact that the course design may provide little opportunity for follow-up work—the next example of the present perfect + "for" may occur some ten units later—and it becomes clear that, though grammatical practice may indeed be given within a functional framework, it is difficult to focus attention on structural concerns in a principled or comprehensive way.

Where such concerns are felt to be important a functional design might better be avoided. High intermediate or advanced students, already familiar with much of the language's grammar, need not suffer from the lack of an organised and graded structural presentation—for such students it is a case of re-representation, rather than initial introduction, of grammatical structures. They will most certainly benefit from the focus on language use afforded by a functional syllabus design, and this may enrich their previous language learning by providing an important "functional dimension".

It might be convincingly argued that at the elementary level, however, a degree of attention should be paid to structural considerations that cannot easily be given within the framework of a functional syllabus. The future may clarify which of a number of possible strategies is suitable: a grammatical approach at the lower levels followed by a functional approach for more advanced students may indeed prove to be the optimal solution. The student would progress from learning how the language operates to learning how it is used, utilising grammatical and functional syllabuses respectively to focus on each task. On the other hand, time may provide evidence that the advantages of presenting language as a system of communication through a functional syllabus— where all the items introduced in one teaching unit have a semantic homogeneity—may even at the elementary level outweigh the disadvantages resulting from the unordered grammatical presentation (which, after all, the child learning its first language learns to cope with successfully). In this situation we might legitimately begin to speak of a "functional method", on a par with audio-visual, audio-lingual and other methods. A third possible solution would indicate that a mixture of structural and functional approaches at the elementary level—with grammatically orientated (components of) units following functional (components of) units—might prove to be efficient.

These remain speculations, however, and where one is concerned not with experimental applied linguistics but with syllabus design affecting the future language learning experience of large groups of students, there seems no responsible alternative to confining the use of functional syllabuses in general courses to the non-elementary levels. At the beginner stage teachers should be sceptical of "abandoning the partly negotiable currency of the grammatical approach for the crock of gold at the end of the functional rainbow" (Wilkins, 1974, p. 120).[3]

Producing Functional Materials

In the present state of the art the task of producing functional materials even at a non-elementary level is not a simple one. Indeed, the appropriate question to ask is the extent to which their rapid and large-scale production (required as the inevitable consequence of any decision to adopt functional syllabuses for general courses taking place in the near future) is at present feasible. Some of the more serious problems, relating to different stages in the process of materials production, are outlined below.

1. Once the decision to adopt a functional approach has been made, a list of the functional headings to be covered has to be drawn up—no mean task if the categories are to be both well-differentiated and suitable as a basis for the production of workable teaching units. A sentence such as "Can you come with me to the cinema tonight?" may in the same context be said simultaneously to fall under a number of categories. At one level it is an exponent of "suggesting a course of action"; at another it is an "invitation"; at yet another it is an "enquiry whether something is considered possible" (all categories in van Ek, 1975). Clearly an enquiry of this latter type may stand as an invitation which, in turn, may form part of a suggestion as to a course of action. But the considerable risk of overlap is only one of the considerations involved here, and great thought needs to be given to the type of category suitable for teaching purposes—categories such as "suggesting a course of action" may well subsume language so diverse and wide-ranging as to make clear peda-gogic presentation difficult; while the language of "enquiring whether something is considered possible" may be so restricted as to be an unsuitable basis for an entire teaching unit. Adoption of categories of this latter type may further prevent important functional generalisations from being made. Is it not an important communicative teaching point to convey that enquiries as to possibility may in English constitute invitations?

The course designer may expect to receive little guidance in this task from other sources. The field of functional syllabus construction is as yet relatively undeveloped, and such work as has been done is of restricted application. The Council of Europe's functional lists (one of which is intended to be merely exemplificatory—Wilkins (1973)—while the other is restricted to a specified level—Van Ek (1975)) are recognised as providing little more than guidelines. The work is moreover firmly rooted in a Western European context, and the applicability of such functional categories to other learning contexts has been brought into question (cf. Widdowson, 1973).

2. At the next stage a decision has to be made concerning which exponents to introduce under each category. This presupposes a knowledge of how the various functions are expounded—knowledge, for example, of how English speakers invite each other to dinner, or ask each other favours. The native speakers will have to rely largely on intuition here, since already prepared lists are scarce—research into the pragmatics of language has simply not reached the degree of development whereby authoritative lists of exponent use may be produced. The non-native speaker, whose own language learning experience has probably been structural and whose exposure to the language used as a system of communication may be severely limited, will find the task particularly daunting.

Even given accurate knowledge of how each function may be expounded, selection from the total exponent lists must still be made. Most functions may be expounded in a large variety of ways: Halliday's (1973)[4] sixteen ways of scolding a child are clearly only a part of the total "semantic network" available for that one function. In the absence of objective information on exponent distribution it is difficult to see how a selection may be other than intuitive and arbitrary.

3. Alternative exponents of the same function, once chosen, will have to be clearly distinguished if adequate materials are to be produced and effective teaching take place. Problems for native and non-native speaker alike are at this stage particularly acute. To select a random example: two of the exponents (justifiably) introduced by van Ek (1975) for the function of *warning* are "Look out." and "Be careful." How are these used? Is it that "Look out." implies an imminent danger, while "Be careful." may warn of a danger in the (even distant) future? Is it true to say that "Look out." is intended to elicit some physical avoiding action, whereas "Be careful." simply alerts the organism to the possibility of danger? To what extent is "Look out." reserved for dangers that are visually perceivable but which have not been noticed—can the expression be used for an invisible yet nevertheless imminent danger? Does

"Look out." imply danger to the addressee himself, rather than his endangering another person or object (as is perhaps (?) suggested by "Mind out.")?

In this particular case the reader may feel confident either that he can distinguish the expressions sufficiently well or that their usage will not cause problems for a particular group of students (perhaps a uni-lingual class whose LI has a similar distinction). But the point is one of frequency: the writer of functional materials aiming to teach what Widdowson (1972) calls the communicative "value" of utterances (and the teacher using such materials) will *constantly* face problems of which this is but one random example. Linguistics may of course ultimately resolve many problems, hopefully providing the course writer with revealing semantic generalisations. But in the present state of knowledge, the danger is that course designers will underestimate the extent of the task required to produce adequate functional materials.

4. There is more to writing functional materials than the simple presentation of selected exponents in functional groupings. Such presentation has the advantage of focusing on the language as a system of communication, and needs to be consolidated by techniques practising the exponents in communicative-like situations. What is required is a fresh consideration of the techniques already available, together with the development of new exercise types. It seems likely that simulation and role play will prove fruitful techniques; but their use in language teaching is as yet relatively new, and it will be several years before the materials developed have stocked a sufficiently large and varied armoury of such techniques to make the large-scale production of adequate functional materials feasible.

The Integration of Functional Materials within Existing Language Teaching Programmes

The difficulties of producing even advanced level functional materials for general courses are therefore many. But what is the proper conclusion to be drawn? Education planners should certainly (because of the difficulties and doubts involved) be wary of adopting functional syllabuses on a large scale, especially when (as is usually the case) decisions once taken cannot be easily reversed. It is also important to realise that the *rapid* production of adequate functional materials is not feasible at the present time. At the very most the gradual and small scale development of such materials is to be recommended.

Equally, going functional—i.e. the *exclusive* adoption of a functional approach, involving the abandonment of familiar methods and techniques already found useful in the given learning situation—is unjustifiable from an applied linguistic, as well as an educational planning, point of view. To claim that any one approach (one syllabus type, one form of practice) may provide for all the multi-dimensional needs of a given nonspecialist language learning group entails unjustifiable theoretical rigidity. Indeed, it is entirely plausible that the most efficient means of providing coverage for specifications such as the Council of Europe's Threshold Level, expressed in terms of functions, settings, topics, notions and structures, is by means of a multi-dimensional set of materials incorporating units of various orientations—functional, notional, structural, etc.[5] Certainly any general course design based on such specifications will need to provide opportunities for practice of a nonfunctional nature, while the principles and aims underlying particular educational programmes will often demand the inclusion of nonfunctional materials.

The conclusion is decidedly *not* that there is no place for functional materials in existing programmes. There can be no doubt that, despite the considerable difficulties involved in their production, such materials can provide an important dimension to language learning, and this is the implicit assumption behind all that has been said. Nor would one advocate a strategy which requires the complete elimination of uncertainties and problems before embarking on course production.

An approach which is both responsible and forward-looking proposes the *gradual*, small-scale development of functional materials, to be *integrated* as one part of already existing programmes. One specific proposal for integration is discussed in Part 2.

Part 2

Background to the Discussion

In 1975 the Yugoslav Republic of Croatia was involved in a wide-ranging curriculum reform covering most aspects of secondary school education. Under this reform, students follow a common programme of study during the first two years of secondary school, and specialise in business, technical, scientific or other subjects during the last two years of the four-year course. Although the third- and fourth-year English programmes embrace a variety of specialisation in this way, it is possible to identify a number of commonly shared language needs providing the basis for a *common core syllabus* which all students, irrespective of specialisation, would be expected to cover during the two years. One required objective of the third- and fourth-year English programme as a whole is to provide a "communicative dimension" to work done within the structurally-based syllabus of the first two years. Indeed, it is seen as a primary aim of any common core materials that they should develop the ability to communicate in everyday conversational interactions, and (as the following discussion makes clear) it is in this area that a functional component would be of potential use. For a detailed description of the Croatian English language teaching situation, see Early (1976).

The present writer was requested to submit proposals to the Croatian authorities concerned in particular with the design of a third- and fourth-year programme to cover specialised as well as common core language needs.[6] The proposals were also intended to consider in general terms the feasibility of a functional approach over the entire language teaching curriculum, including the elementary level; but for the reasons given in Part I relating to the question of functional syllabuses and level, this type of approach was thought to be inappropriate at the elementary level.

Many of the details in these proposals are of local interest only, and discussion here is restricted to considerations of what form any common core materials (intended to provide the kind of "general course" discussed in Part I) should take, and of how a functional component might be integrated within them. What the functional component might look like (in terms of types of practice offered, techniques used, etc.) is not considered in detail here.

The Existing Framework and its Suitability as a Basis for Producing Common Core Materials

The standard of materials production in Croatia is high, and texts suitable for secondary school use are available from a number of sources. Recently the Education Department has favoured an approach using materials organised around what might be called "theme areas". Examples of such theme areas are: "Red Indians", "the generation gap", "a holiday in London", "a railway station". Associated with each are sets of teaching materials including passages of prose, poems, dialogues, song texts, etc., on clusters of topics related to the central theme areas. These "source texts" provide the stimulus for several weeks' language work utilising a variety of techniques including project work, group work, role play, discussions. The framework is a loose one, and the materials are often related to the central theme areas only in indirect ways. Thus mention of a newspaper kiosk under the "railway station" theme area may lead to the introduction of source texts about the press, followed by project work and discussions on the subject.

Structural practice, comprehension exercises, pronunciation drilling and other forms of what will be referred to below as "language practice materials" are at present partly provided by ancillary books such as O'Neill (1973), and partly by exercises built into the theme area framework as follow-ups to the source texts.

The theme area approach has a number of advantages which argue for its retention under the new syllabus, especially given some of the specific objectives and principles of the Croatian Education Department. Part of its pedagogic attraction is that as a mode of presentation it has considerable "face validity". The students may easily relate the selected topics to their own interests, and whereas they might feel a functional or structural link between materials presented in the same unit to be somewhat contrived and "abstract", they are likely to find the thematic link both natural and immediately perceivable.[7] The approach also provides ample exposure to the language through the numerous source texts which, since they inevitably contain many points of linguistic interest, serve as an excellent point of departure for subsequent exercises. In this way the language to be practised is first introduced in rich communicative contexts rather than in isolated "key sentences" or specially written dialogues.

The Education Department places great emphasis on the need to familiarise students with the life and culture of native-speaker communities. The theme area approach has provided an excellent vehicle for conveying cultural information, and the source materials contain a wealth of sociolinguistic detail. At the practice stage, project work (which for a variety of reasons is a favoured technique) often involves the students themselves in exploring aspects of the native speaker culture. In addition, the approach is both multi-media and multi-disciplinary. The somewhat loose framework of the theme area permits easy integration of materials on film, slides, tapes and records, while points of historical, geographical, sociological, etc. interest arise out of the source texts and are followed up in project work. In these respects the approach is in keeping with the general principles of the Education Department.

The major potential shortcoming of the approach lies in its suitability for developing proficiency at communication in conversational inter-actions. A theme-based approach making extensive use of project work runs the risk of overemphasising the "language of reporting" (describing, narrating). It may encourage the students to talk—to describe railway stations, to narrate events from history, to report the findings of project work—but the practice tends (though the course writers have attempted to counteract this tendency by the introduction of simulation exercises) to involve the construction of extended monologues on subjects of cultural relevance. The interactive skills necessary for conversational proficiency—the ability to respond quickly and appropriately (along ideational, interpersonal and textual parameters) to utterances whose content and form are not known in advance—involve elements not required for acts of reporting, describing, narrating, and a qualitative different kind of practice is required.

But there is a "quantitative" as well as a "qualitative" point to be made. Reporting, describing and narrating account for a small part of everyday interactions, and if conversational ability is to be developed, a wider range of language functions must be dealt with—not just describing, reporting, narrating, but also greeting, inviting, apologising, etc. Similarly, extensive coverage must be given in terms of settings and topics. As it stands, the approach is likely to provide relatively thorough coverage of a small number of theme areas. Materials on the theme area of railway stations, for example, might produce in the students an impressive knowledge of, and expertise to handle situations concerned with, rail transport; the danger is that the framework which permits such thorough treatment of selected themes will fail to deal with a range of settings and topics sufficiently extensive to meet the students' language needs. In this situation the type of approach proposed by the Council of Europe team is particularly useful. The procedures advocated by Richterich (1973) and exemplified by van Ek (1975) provide the means of "quantifying" language use in relationship to the known language needs of the student population. Such procedures find clear application in this situation, where it is a question of ensuring adequate coverage of a wide range of functions, settings and topics.

Proposed Framework for Common Core Materials

Despite potential shortcomings, the existing framework remains pedagogically attractive, and the materials produced within it well serve a number of the Education Department's aims. Rejection of framework and materials in favour of an exclusively functional approach, which might meet the single objective of providing a communicative dimension in a more efficient way, would clearly be ill advised. Equally clearly, however, a functional *component* integrated within the existing framework would ensure that due emphasis is given to communicative considerations.

Under such a scheme coverage of the common core might be provided by a series of teaching units each containing theme-specific and language practice materials (following the already established patterns described earlier) alongside materials with a functional orientation. Each unit would cover a separate theme area, and the theme-specific source texts would serve as the point of departure for both language practice and functional materials. To this extent the theme area mode of presentation now used would be retained.

There seems no reason why a specific sequence for the presentation of the three material types within each unit need be fixed, though the fact that the source texts are to provide the stimulus for language practice and functional materials will clearly impose some restrictions on the ordering. Nor should the material types necessarily appear as separate parts of the unit: it would be possible (for example) to move from theme-specific materials to what has been called "language practice", return to theme-specific followed by functional materials, ending up with more language practice.

The Scope of the Functional Component, and its Relationship to Other Materials

A potential disadvantage of this "multi-dimensional" framework, where materials of differing orientations are presented together in the same unit, is that the students will find themselves confused by the frequent shifts in focus. It is therefore pedagogically desirable that the heterogeneous materials should be seen to be linked together in some way. Choice of the "theme area mode of presentation", in which both functional and language practice materials use the rich context of the theme-specific source texts as their starting point, provides such a link.

But what should the nature of the link be, and by what criteria should one decide to associate a particular function with a given theme area? Should "making arrangements" be introduced in the "railway station" or the "holiday in London" theme area, for example? Certainly the source texts in both are likely to provide examples of arrangements being made, any of which might be used as a stimulus for functional practice. In fact, consideration of all the functions to be covered in relation to all the selected theme areas is not likely to reveal persuasive arguments in favour of one set of associations rather than any other. No "natural links" will suggest themselves, and to this extent the selection of which function to link with which theme is of little importance.

This does not mean that the ordering of the themes and functions within the course shall be arrived at in an arbitrary way. There will certainly be valid criteria for sequencing the functions, and to a less extent the themes, in particular ways over the course as a whole. Criteria for functional sequencing are discussed elsewhere in this volume;[8] as regards themes, it may be decided to deal with "means of transport" in a block of units, one of which is concerned with the "railway station" theme area. In this way, following a principled procedure, the "railway station" theme and the "making arrangements" function might fall together in the same unit; but the association in itself has no significance.

The reason why no "natural links" between themes and functions suggest themselves is of course simply that functions are largely "non-setting-specific": thus we may *persuade* (*invite, make arrangements with*) many kinds of people to do many sorts of things in many different settings, and indeed it must be seen as a primary aim of the functional component to practise each function in relation to the various settings and topics which the syllabus would specify. This is important not simply to provide a counterbalance to the relative restriction of settings and topics in the theme-specific materials, but also to indicate each function's full scope of application—something which a number of recently pro-duced "functional" coursebooks markedly fail to do. Indeed, to present settings and functions in a one-to-one relationship would be either to reflect a fundamental misconception on the part of the materials pro-ducer concerning the nature of language use, or an unacceptable degree of simplification for pedagogic purposes.[9]

There is another reason why a relatively "weak" link between function and theme is desirable: to create too strong an association would be to make the essential task of generalising function out of initial context of presentation that much harder. Thus while the function of "requesting information or services", for example, might be introduced under the theme area of "railway station" (perhaps through a dialogue in which a traveller requests the services of a porter) the students' attention would rapidly be directed to other sorts of requests, made in hotels, restaurants, school and business life—for rooms, meals, advice, secretarial assistance, etc. In this way the functional component uses the theme-specific materials as little more than a starting point, and ranges far beyond them into non-theme-specific settings and topics.

The motivations for linking functional (and language practice) ma-terials to the theme-specific source texts are pedagogic: the latter provide excellent contexts for initial presentation, while the fact that the ma-terials are linked together gives a coherence to the unit as a whole. But the course writer clearly has to strike a delicate balance between these pedagogic requirements and the necessity for the functional component to indicate the functions' scope of application over a wide range of settings and topics.

Conclusion

The Croatian situation provides an example of a case where exclusive adoption of a functional approach would be undesirable in the light of the effective alternative teaching methods developed over the years. Yet there is an argument in favour of adding a "functional component" to counteract certain potential deficiencies in the existing programme. The argument here has been in favour of a relatively weak link between functional and other types of language practice, a major consideration being to ensure that coverage of the functions is not restricted to the settings and topics in relation to which they are first introduced.

Notes

1. Thanks are due to David Wilkins and Keith Morrow for comments on a draft of this paper.
2. For discussion of the application of functional syllabuses for "special" types of courses, see Paper 9. See also discussion in Paper 3 on the Council of Europe's concept of the "common core".
3. The first two of these solutions imply the different theoretical positions discussed in Paper 1, pp. 21–22. The question of semantic syllabuses and beginner students is discussed at length in Paper 8.
4. This paper of Halliday's is described in Paper 1.
5. The concept of "multi-dimensionality" is discussed at length in Paper 4.
6. These proposals are outlined in Johnson (1975).
7. This difference between setting/topic-based materials and functional/notional materials is discussed in Paper 4.
8. In Paper 5.
9. A similar point is made in Paper 6 concerning the relationship between communicative function and discourse position.

Paper 8:

Adult Beginners: a Functional or a Communicative Structural Approach?

This paper looks at the question of whether a functional syllabus is appropriate for the adult beginner student. It is highly polemic in tone, and part of its intention was to stimulate debate on the subject at a time when a number of apparently functional beginner materials were about to appear on the market. The paper proposes a "communicative structural" alternative where the "communicative" element is supplied by the methodology. In this way the paper anticipates Sections 3 and 4 where two of the recurring themes are firstly that there are doubts concerning the validity of semantic syllabuses for any course design; and second that whether or not a course is "communicative" will depend as much on its methodology as on the pedigree of its syllabus.

This paper was delivered at the Annual General Meeting of the British Association for Applied Linguistics, held at Colchester in September, 1977 (the year in which it was written). A simplified version of it appeared in Modern English Teacher, **6**, 2, 1978, *and in various other European journals.*

THE AIM of this paper is to question the desirability of semantic—and particularly functional—syllabuses at the zero beginner level, and to argue that a beginners' course may be designed structurally and at the same time incorporate many valuable features associated with the approach to language teaching which is nowadays called "communicative".

There is one central and persuasive argument against the use of functional syllabuses at the zero beginner level. It is simply that a functional organisation automatically implies structural disorganisation.[1] Many would argue that for an adult beginner learning the foreign language in the classroom, the language system needs to be presented in a graded progression so that the learner may perceive and practise structural regularities one by one. Counterarguments against this position would have, presumably, to show either that functional syllabuses need not imply serious structural disorganisation, or that structural disorganisation may not be a disadvantage. In fact most of the arguments in favour of beginner functional syllabuses are of a different sort. They point to deficiencies in structural syllabuses and claim that these deficiencies are not present in functional designs. Structural syllabuses, they say, have such and such disadvantages, which functional syllabuses do not have. My lawn mower is broken, but my electric razor isn't; so I'll use my electric razor to cut the lawn. The argument to be developed here is a different one: structural syllabuses in the past may have had disadvantages; therefore we have to try and improve them. My lawn mower is broken, so I'll try to mend it.

A common argument against structural syllabuses is that (and the quotation is verbatim from someone involved in semantic materials production for zero beginners) "they do not allow you to see the practical applications of the language to real life." There are three possible things that may be implied here. One is that in a structural syllabus we teach the wrong language. That is, our selection of the language items to teach—structures and lexis—is incorrect given the eventual language needs of our students. We are teaching language that simply has no application in real life situations.

It is certainly true that one fundamental criterion for deciding whether or not a given item should be included in a course is its communicative utility to the student. If the analysis of language needs reveals that an item is highly uncommon for the student's usual communicative purposes, then this is argument enough for omission of the item, always assuming (and this is a further criterion) that its acquisition is not a vital stepping stone for the acquisition of some other, communicatively important, structure. It is certainly also true that the structural coursewriter occasionally becomes overzealous in his desire to make the syllabus a comprehensive survey of the language's grammar, and this may lead to the inclusion of structures which, on the grounds of utility, might better be omitted. Where this is clearly the case, then the solution is simple, and does not involve changing the orientation of the syllabus design from structural to semantic. It is to omit the offending structure from the course. But the extent to which the criterion of communicative utility is likely to change the structural content of language courses is probably small. The structures listed in a comprehensive semantic syllabus inventory (drawn up along the lines of van Ek, 1975) will probably be more or less those found in more conventional syllabus inventories. The *way* in which the structures are listed will certainly be different—in the semantic inventory they will be classified according to the notions and functions they may perform, while in traditional inventories the lists are made according to structural features. But the structures themselves will be more or less the same. This is not really surprising. Though the language system may be used to generate an infinite number of sentences, it is in itself a finite construct. So lists of the structural items comprising the system will be extremely similar, by whatever criteria they are drawn up.

A similar argument holds for lexis. Doubtless one can find many structural courses where the choice of lexis is far from felicitous. But this is easily rectified. If the analysis of language needs reveals that lexical items such as "truck", "bulldozer", "tractor" are more useful for a given group of students than "car", "train", "boat", then we simply include the former and eliminate the latter. There is certainly no motivation here for changing to a semantic syllabus.

"Structural syllabuses do not allow you to see the practical applications of the language to real life." A second thing that might be implied here is that although structural syllabuses teach the right language items, they often introduce them in the wrong situations (using this word to refer to the entire matrix of contextual features) and being employed for the wrong function. This is certainly a valid criticism. We are all familiar with materials in which the characters' breakfast-time conversation consists of sequences like "Is this a table?", "Yes, it is."; "Is this a chair?", "No, it isn't."; and who, at the slightest provocation inform us that "The green book is under the chair." or "John's pen is near the book." The structures in these sentences are the right ones to teach—no-one would claim that interrogatives and short form answers using "be", prepositional phrases and the rest, have no application to real life! What we rightly object to is the total inappropriacy of such sentences to the situations in which they are supposed to be uttered. Structural courses are indeed often "situationally dishonest"; but they need not be so. Since these structures do have applications in real life, it should take no effort (and at the very most a little ingenuity) to find situations in which they can be used with absolute appropriacy. The solution to situational dishonesty is not to turn the syllabus topsy turvy. All that is needed is care in the selection of the situations in which the structures we wish to teach are uttered.[2]

Apart from being "situationally dishonest", structural courses are also often functionally dishonest. They often illustrate sentences functioning in unreal ways, while at the same time failing to illustrate the common functions which structures expound. Widdowson's (1972) example of this type of failure concerns the common procedure for teaching the present continuous tense, in relation to the function of commentary—a rather rare function in itself and quite unnatural in the classroom situation.[3] But there are plenty of situations in which we can introduce the present continuous used in functionally appropriate ways, and the best structural coursebooks do this.

The point being made is that we can advocate situational and functional honesty without this implying adoption of a semantic syllabus design. In the same way that we would expect a functional course to be structurally accurate—to contain, that is, language which is grammatically accurate—so it seems reasonable to expect our structural courses to exemplify language being used to correct purpose in appropriate situations.

When people say that a structural approach does not allow students to see the practical applications of the language to real life, a third thing they may mean is that the approach fails to draw these applications to the students' attention in an explicit way. So that when we teach structures such as "Would you like to . . .?" we may not explicitly point out to the students that a common use of this structure is to invite, even though some examples of this structure may clearly be invitations. One can argue very strongly that at *some* level explicit attention needs to be paid to use. It is a question of when this should be done; and at the zero beginner level there is much to be said for focusing attention on structure. But to repeat (at the risk of being tedious): we do not have to lie. We can be functionally honest without being functionally explicit.

A further set of arguments against structural syllabuses also concerns the relationship between language taught and its application to real life. Some say that structural syllabuses fail to differentiate between structures of high and low frequency, in two ways. The first is in the amount of time devoted to them. Structural materials may spend as much time teaching the passive as they spend on teaching the past tense, even though the latter may be more frequent than the former in normal communicative situations. The criteria used to decide how much time to spend on an item is, in other words, its supposed structural difficulty rather than its frequency of occurrence. But in fact this seems a not unreasonable criterion to adopt. If something is easy (whatever its frequency of occurrence) then little time *need* be devoted to it, and if something is difficult (again, whatever its frequency of occurrence), then more time *must* be devoted to it. To claim that less time should be spent teaching something difficult because it is not often used is tantamount to condoning its imperfect teaching. Infrequency of occurrence with reference to the students' language needs may be a criterion for omitting a structure from a teaching programme, but once the decision to include a structure has been made, then supposed difficulty of acquisition seems a more valid criterion for deciding how much time should be spent on teaching it.

The second way in which a structural syllabus may fail to differentiate between structural items of high and low frequency is in the point at which they are introduced. By following a graded grammatical progression the structural syllabus may well find itself spending time on less frequent structures while having to delay the introduction of communicatively more important ones. This argument is often heard in relation to tenses such as the simple past or the present perfect, the introduction of which may appear to be unreasonably delayed in many courses. There can be a justifiable reason or an unjustifiable reason for delays of this sort. The justifiable reason is simply the belief that structural grading remains the most efficient means we have for presenting the language to the learner. It is surely quite valid to delay introduction of the simple past tense, for example, if we believe that the student can only master it when he understands how the auxiliary system using "do" is employed to form interrogatives and negatives; how the contraction system, short answer forms and the like are constructed. If the advocates of semantic syllabuses for zero beginners believe that the simple past should be introduced early, would they do so before those essential preliminaries have been mastered? If so, they surely run the risk that the student will simply fail to acquire the form, and the haste for communicative competence will result in pedagogic incompetence.

The unjustifiable reason for delay would simply be that the syllabus designer has arrived at his ordering not because he believes it to be the most cost-effective means of assuring acquisition, but simply because he is following the order found in the work of a descriptive linguist. Justifications for a particular ordering which run "we've taught the present, so now we'll move on to the past" or "we've done the indicative, so now we'll do the imperative" are not justifications at all. They smack of a taxonomic linguistic description made without regard for either communicative needs or structural complexity. The functional syllabus designer can of course make the same mistake. He may decide to teach his functions in the same order as they are listed in the syllabus inventory, with no more motive for the ordering than the fact that the inventory lists them in that way. When the structural materials designer does err here, the answer is simply a reappraisal. We should look again at our structural lists and move forward any communicatively important items which can be taught early without destroying the structural progression necessary for acquisition to take place in the most cost-effective way. It is difficult to know how much re-ordering this reappraisal might feasibly entail—one suspects not much. But it does seem to be a more apposite answer to the problem than simply "going semantic".

So far the arguments considered against the adoption of grammatical syllabuses have been concerned with the selection and ordering of structures. Another set of arguments revolves around the claim that structural syllabuses have "low surrender value", because the student often has to study for several years before he gets any pay-off in terms of communicative ability.[4] Incidentally—and this is not the central point being made here—high surrender value is only useful, both in insurance and in language teaching, when the return on investment does indeed need to be swift. In language teaching this is particularly the case in short-term remedial courses where the students have restricted time to study the language. But no beginners' course is of this type.[5] These are usually written for audiences assumed to have an extended period of time at their disposal for learning the language. There is generally no *external* pressure demanding a course with high surrender value. It pays to remember that there exist insurance policies with low surrender value, and that it is on these that the eventual return on investment is the most secure.

There is, however, an *internal* pressure on every sort of course for a high surrender value. Little wonder—a far more persuasive argument runs—if students lose interest in learning a language if three or more years pass before they are given any practice in using the language as a system of communication, rather than simply learning it as an unapplied set of rules. But can communicative practice only be given in a semantic syllabus? Does adoption of a grammatical design automatically condemn the students to endless structural drills which have no communicative value? The answer to both these questions is surely no. There are certainly courses on the market which, though semantic in design, give no communicative practice at all. They are simply elaborate phrasebooks which tell the students what to say and when to say it, without providing them with any practice in operating within communicative situations. Language being taught as an unapplied system! Similarly, there are structural courses available which contain exercises of great communicative value. The students pass on messages to each other which have actual communicative content; they ask each other questions the answers to which they do not already know; they are made to utilise information received in the course of an interaction to some further purpose.[6] Communicative language teaching need not be the same thing as functional language teaching. We can make our exercises as meaningful—or as meaningless—in a unit about the present perfect as we can in a unit about *inviting*. If communicative practice is what gives a course high surrender value, then this can be achieved in a structural as well as a functional syllabus.

Now to change the emphasis. So far the suggestion has been that so-called shortcomings in structural syllabuses can be overcome—where in fact they are shortcomings at all—without resorting to the use of semantic syllabuses at the zero beginner level. By way of summary, and looking at the issue from a more positive point of view, it may be useful to restate some of the ways in which a structural syllabus may take advantage of recent developments in language teaching, and become more communicative. How may a structural syllabus be communicative?

One of the most important advances in recent years associated with communicative language teaching is that we now look at student language needs in a way which is both aggressive and multi-dimensional. It is aggressive in the sense that we now seriously pose the question "what do our students want to use the language for?", and make the answer affect the actual content of our course. If we ask what effects this new aggression is likely to have on the *structural* content of an adult beginner course, then the answer is likely to be very little. We may find that a certain amount of re-ordering of structures is necessary, and to the extent that this may be done without affecting the structural grading which most believe is necessary for acquisition to take place, it can and should be done. We may also find it possible to drop certain structures altogether, the communicative utility of which is small. Such a reconsideration of structural syllabuses in terms of communicative need cannot but be beneficial. But what the new aggression will affect most is the *uses* to which the structures introduced are put, the *settings* they are introduced in, and the *topics* they are used to talk about. From these points of view all coursewriters (whether they are writing structurally or semantically orientated materials) must be aggressive. The days of breakfast-time conversations about tables and chairs, and long classroom commentaries on student actions should, we might feel, be banished for ever. But they can surely be banished without radical changes in syllabus design.

Our way of listing student language needs is now multi-dimensional because whereas before syllabuses were based on structural and lexical lists alone, they are now based on inventories which also consider functions, notions, settings and so on. The specifications today are richer, more complex, and because such specifications may lead to structural as well as semantic syllabuses, this poses a challenge to all syllabus designers whatever their orientation. Since these specifications identify student needs in a more precise manner, the result will be more useful courses whether they are semantically or structurally organised.[7]

The structural coursewriter, then, can and should develop his materials within the framework of a semantic syllabus inventory. Similarly, he may benefit from recent developments in methodology. It is certainly too early to talk in terms of an established communicative methodology, but certain trends are discernible. One is the development of exercises involving the student in situations where there is a true "information gap".[8] Students may, for example, be given small tasks which can only be undertaken if a certain amount of information is made available. Other members of the class are placed in a position to provide this information. With a little ingenuity it is possible to arrange that the language practised in such exercises is structurally homogeneous, while at the same time ensuring that the utterances produced are both situationally and functionally appropriate.

Notes

1. This point is amplified in Paper 7. See particularly pages 92–3.
2. Paper 14 examines the question of "situational dishonesty" in relation to a concrete example.
3. Widdowson's example is discussed in more detail in Paper 1.
4. The concept of surrender value is further discussed in Papers 6 and 9.
5. Dick Allwright has pointed out (in discussion) that this is not strictly true; there are beginners' courses where there is a demand for swift return on investment. Wilkins (1974) recognises that high surrender value is not required in all situations.
6. These aspects of a communicative methodology are considered in detail in Section 4 of this book.
7. The word multi-dimensional is used in a different sense in Paper 4 with reference to syllabus rather than syllabus inventory. On the claim that semantic syllabus inventories can lead to structural syllabuses, see Paper 4 also.
8. For detailed discussion of the information gap, see Papers 13 and 14. Paper 14 contains an example of an exercise type which might occur in a "communicative structural" approach.

Paper 9:

Functional Syllabuses for Remedial and Short-Term Courses

Two possible areas of application claimed for the functional syllabus are on remedial and short-term courses. The aim of this short paper is to pose a number of questions concerning these claims.[1] Like previous papers it expresses many doubts and therefore looks towards Section 3. In its early pages it makes a distinction between what are called "weak" and "strong" claims for the notional syllabus. This important distinction (already touched on in Paper 1) is also to recur in Section 3, particularly in Paper 11.

This paper is a shortened version of one which appeared in Johnson & Morrow (1978).

Remedial Teaching

THE ARGUMENT in favour of a functional syllabus for remedial teaching runs as follows: the remedial course is for students who have already followed one (structural) course, and have failed to learn properly. Hitherto the strategy has basically been one of repetition: the students either repeat the course or follow a similar one. This is likely to be a tedious process at the very least; and since the structural course did not succeed the first time round, it may well be expected to fail again. Use of a functional syllabus in this situation, the argument runs, will provide re-exposure to grammar, but within a different kind of framework.

How convincing is the argument? Are we simply saying, in desperation, that we have failed with one method and will therefore (as part of a process of trial and error) adopt another? Or are there really grounds for assuming that, having failed to learn *structures* in a *structural* course, the student will learn *structures* in a *functional* course? There is a "weak" and a "strong" claim which may be made for the functional syllabus.[2] The weak claim would argue that the functional syllabus provides an additional dimension to teaching. The structural syllabus teaches the "rules of grammar", and the functional syllabus the "rules of use"—both being necessary for mastery of the language. In this sense the functional syllabus adds to rather than replaces the structural syllabus. According to a strong claim the language system is best taught in relation to "meanings" or "uses", and should therefore be seen as a replacement of, rather than as an addition to, the structural syllabus.[3] The assumption that the student will acquire structures in a functional remedial course would seem to involve a claim of the strong type. And if it is true that functional syllabuses teach structure better than structural syllabuses, then surely our initial teaching should be functional. There would presumably then be no need for remediation!

It may be true that a change of emphasis is likely to ward off the tedium which is the potential danger inherent in remedial teaching, though this says nothing interesting about the functional syllabus. The functional syllabus may well work remedially simply by virtue of the fact that it is different from the approach that the students are used to, and tired of.

Short-Term Courses

It is in connection with this type of course that the term "high surrender value" is most often mentioned.[4] In a situation where the students have two or three months to reach a given standard of English for a given purpose, there are at least three strategies open to the teacher. One is to work through a part of the grammar, covering as many units as possible of a structural coursebook. The coverage will be incomplete and the structures learned will not necessarily be the important ones—merely those that happen to occur in the units studied. A second possibility is to try and provide the student with a general "overview" of how the language operates, by covering the main structures. This solution is undoubtedly better (though perhaps less common) than the first since the structures are at least selected according to some principle. In the third strategy we would identify and teach important areas of functional use.

Given that all short-term courses are certain to be incomplete (and hence in some way unsatisfactory), it is important to be clear what the various approaches may and may not be expected to achieve. The first two solutions aim to provide a degree of structural competence. The result is likely to be students who are able to produce a (restricted) number of grammatical sentences, which they may not be able to put to appropriate use. We will have given some of the basics necessary for communication; but the student will have to devote more time to learning before he reaps the full value of his "investment". We might even wish to argue that, provided with these basics, the student will easily learn to be appropriate as he operates in the native speaker environment. At the end of the functional course the student will have a "phrasebook" to help him with vital needs, and the benefit he reaps from learning is likely to be immediate. But he may lack the grammatical foundation to generalise and apply what he has learned outside the "phrasebook situation". The choice is thus: either we provide as thorough a grounding of the language system as possible, and leave the student to learn how to apply that system himself; or we meet his immediate needs, but in the knowledge that what is taught is highly restricted in its area of application.[5]

With the issue expressed in these terms we would need to look carefully at the students' particular circumstances before advocating one or another approach. How much grammatical knowledge can be assumed? If a lot, then the restricted time available might be best spent in teaching its "use". How restricted is the need for English? Perhaps a highly limited phrasebook is all that is required. How long will the students remain in the country? Will they have the time and the opportunity to learn how to apply any grammatical foundation provided in a course? As these questions suggest, it cannot be automatically assumed that in all short-term teaching situations the functional syllabus provides the best solution.

Notes

1. See particularly Wilkins (1974) on the use of semantic syllabuses in these situations.
2. These claims are related to their theoretical background in Paper 1. See page 22. See also Paper 11.
3. Prabhu's claim in Paper 12 is similar, but it does not lead him to the functional syllabus.
4. For example in Wilkins (1974). See Papers 6 and 8 for more detailed discussion of the concept of surrender value.
5. The important topic of "generativity", touched on in this paragraph, reoccurs in a somewhat disguised form in Papers 11 and 19.

Section 3:

SYLLABUS DESIGN: TOWARDS A NEW APPROACH

Paper 10:

Two Approaches to the Teaching of Communication

Previous papers have expressed a number of doubts concerning the semantic syllabus. But the basis validity of the approach has not been seriously questioned (see for example the comments in Paper 7, page 91). This is not true in Paper 10. Like the other papers in this section, it is theoretical; it also has a central place in the collection because it deals with both syllabus design and methodology. There have, the paper claims, been two quite distinct approaches to communicative language teaching, one primarily concerned with syllabus design and the other with methodology. It argues that a coherent approach must bring these two areas together, and that the "notional" approach fails to do this.

The paper is the first part of one entitled "Communicative approaches and communicative processes" which appears in Brumfit and Johnson (1979).

Much of the very considerable momentum of present day language teaching may be seen as a response to a problem which teachers have been aware of for a long time. It is the problem of the student who may be structurally competent, but who cannot communicate appropriately. As Newmark (1966) expresses it, this student may know

> the structures that the linguist teaches, [yet] cannot know that the way to get his cigarette lit by a stranger when he has no matches is to walk up to him and say one of the utterances "Do you have a light?" or "Got a match?" (not one of the equally well-formed questions "Do you have a fire?" or "Do you have illumination?" or "Are you a match's owner?").

Language teaching's most concerted response to this problem has been on the level of syllabus design, through the development of the semantic syllabus. So much so that when we speak of "communicative language teaching" we are (in common usage) referring to one which, recognising the necessity for teaching use, bases itself on inventories specifying conceptual and pragmatic categories which are arrived at by considering presumed communicative needs. The approach proposes what might be called a "teaching content" solution to the problem of communicative incompetence. Applied to the particular instance Newmark cites, it is a solution which might account for the student's ignorance of how to ask for a light by the delightfully simple fact that items like "asking for a light" have not formed part of our teaching content. Once we conceive our teaching in terms which embrace categories of use (including the general *requesting services* and the particular "asking for a light") then—this type of solution seems to be proposing— the major step to solving the problem has been taken. Of course it is recognised that the decision to teach language in relation to categories of use is likely to have methodological implications; but they are implications which follow and are contingent upon our prior decision, made at the syllabus planning level, to specify teaching content in a particular "semantic" way.

Given the predominance of the "teaching content" solution in recent teaching, it is all the more interesting to note that it is not at all obviously the solution that Newmark himself proposes. Newmark does have things to say about the specification of teaching content but both his diagnosis and his treatment have a methodological base. According to him, the illness exists because we have failed to realise that "acquisition cannot be simply additive; complex bits of language are learned a whole chunk at a time." Consequently his recommended treatment is to exploit the "exponential power available in learning in natural chunks." This "methodologically-based" solution is one which appeals because it seems potentially to offer an alternative to aspects of traditional methodology which have long caused widespread discontent and which, in the eyes of many, are responsible for communicative incompetence—aspects like painfully slow incremental teaching, the drilling of language items in isolation, and so on. It is also a type of solution which is gaining support today, and we are beginning to find approaches to communicative language teaching which share in common a greater concern with issues of methodology than with the specification of syllabus content. One such approach is discussed by Brumfit (1979) who suggests that the trad-itional sequence of "present→drill→practice in context" is being re-placed by a strategy in which the students first communicate as far as possible with available resources, and are then presented with language items shown to be necessary—these items being drilled if appropriate.[1]

We have, then, a situation in which there are effectively two ways of accounting for communicative incompetence, two types of proposed solution to the problem. Are there then two types of communicative language teaching? There certainly seem to be in practice two broad approaches. One is characterised by the rigorous specification of com-municative needs typical of much ESP work, but often coupled with a methodology which is not significantly unlike traditional methodology. The other proposes methodological procedures that are quite often revolutionary, but equally often remain uncommitted on questions of syllabus design. It is a situation that certainly prompts us to ask what the relationship between the two approaches is, what the methodological implications of the "teaching content" solution are, and what the methodologically-based solutions imply in terms of syllabus design.

Attempts have certainly been made to link the two approaches to-gether. Indeed, at times Newmark (with his "methodological approach") makes statements which suggest that he would look with favour on the kind of precise semantic terms in which most teaching content solutions express themselves. This is particularly true when he laments the lack of precision in the specification of categories of use, and notes that "the kinds of linguistic rules that have been characterised so far . . . bear on questions of well-formedness of sentences, not on questions of appropriateness of utterances". We need more rules, he seems to be saying, but of a different type. Rules, perhaps, that can eventually be incorporated into syllabuses? Wilkins' attempt to link the two types of approach (1976) is more explicit. He draws a distinction between "synthe-tic" and "analytic" teaching strategies, a distinction which has much in common with the one Newmark is making, and the one between traditional methodologies on the one hand and the kind of "method-ological solution" we have been considering here on the other. In a synthetic approach the teacher isolates and orders the forms of the linguistic system, systematically presents them to the student one by one and thus incrementally builds up language competence. In analytic teaching it is the student who does the analysis from data presented to him in the form of "natural chunks". Wilkins associates the synthetic approach with structural syllabuses, and the analytic with notional specifications.

One—if not the—central feature of Newmark's standpoint is that "consideration of the details supplied by ... analysis has taken away from the exponential power available in learning in natural chunks"; that, in other words, the whole machinery of linguistic paraphernalia which we employ in teaching (particularly, one might think, in the specification of teaching content) constitutes an interference with the language learning process. At many points in Wilkins' discussion he seems to be leading towards a similar conclusion—that what is wrong with the synthetic approach is teacher pre-selection and isolation of items, and that this in some way does not happen with the analytic approach. It is with the distinction made in this way that we are able to make a clear-cut methodological differentiation between the strategies, and are able to give the kind of coherent psycholinguistic justification for the analytic that Newmark hints at, making reference to the process of first language acquisition. One might indeed argue that it is only with the distinction made thus that we can meaningfully claim to be "basing our approach on the learner's analytic capacities" (Wilkins, 1976, p. 14), something which seems to necessitate the degree of student control over teaching content that solutions like Brumfit's (with its "initial communication with available resources") appears to imply. It is certainly difficult to see how an approach which condones and actively attempts to practise teacher pre-selection/isolation, and whose claim to "analycity" rests only in that it presents the pre-selected and isolated items in "natural chunks" can rely in any sense on the student's analytic capacities, or distinguish itself sufficiently from most so-called synthetic teaching to be worthy of another name.

We can argue, then, quite strongly, that a truly analytic approach should entail lack of teacher pre-selection and isolation of items. But what does this imply in terms of syllabus design? Is the implication that syllabuses, as the explicit formulation and pre-selection by the teacher of teaching content, should not be drawn up at all? Certainly Newmark's observations concerning the interference caused by "the details supplied by ... analysis" (together with the types of methodological solution being proposed nowadays) appear to entail at the very least a de-emphasis of the importance of syllabus design. But if de-emphasis (rather than abolition), then how does this manifest itself? What does a "de-emphasised syllabus" look like? These general questions lead to specific ones, such as how we decide on (i.e. pre-select) what the "initial communication with available resources" in Brumfit's solution is to be communication about.[2]

Wilkins' answer is neither the abolition nor the de-emphasis of the syllabus. It is rather to draw a qualitative distinction between the formulation of teaching content in structural and in semantic terms. His claim is that semantic specification, because it is "behavioural" rather than "linguistic", is essentially part of an analytic strategy. But it is difficult to see how, once we are prepared to commit ourselves to entering into the process of specification (in whatever terms) we can fail to arrive at a syllabus content which is either explicitly linguistic or will implicitly shape the linguistic content of our teaching. As Wilkins (1976, p. 13) admits: "since it is language behaviour we are concerned with, it is possible, indeed desirable, that the linguistic content of any unit [in semantic teaching materials] should also be stated", implying that the difference between semantic and structural syllabuses is merely that the former has a behavioural underpinning that the latter lacks. The difference is in starting point, less clearly in final result. Certainly the amount of attention that has been paid to questions of syllabus design in the past few years and the development of tools such as Munby's (1978) intended to make our specifications as "scientific", precise and detailed as possible seem to violate the very spirit of Newmark's "minimal strategy", and the belief that analysis interferes with acquisition. Certainly also many of the materials which have been produced following semantic syllabuses indicate that this type of specification *can* lead to synthetic teaching. Indeed, if one argues that any detailed specification of teaching content (albeit made in semantic rather than, initially, structural terms) is synthetic, then one is forced to the conclusion that semantic syllabuses are *a priori* synthetic constructs which not only admit, but also invite or even impose a synthetic strategy.

By way of conclusion: the kind of difficulties discussed here reflect a basic and perhaps unresolvable conflict between teacher and student control. In the reading of the present situation given above, some form of "student control" is taken as central to the concept of analycity. In these terms, the "methodological solutions" can lay more claim to analycity, though it does remain unclear whether (and if so, to what degree and in what form) they condone teacher control by pre-selection of content. But exactly because they are sufficiently recognisable as analytic, they give rise to a further question: the extent to which they can convince as general strategies for language teaching rather than merely as language activation procedures for advanced students. If, in other words, we accept them as analytic, we have still to determine whether analycity works.

There are two ways of viewing the semantic "teaching content" solution. One is an attempt to be analytic that failed. The other is to regard its main mistake as the attempt to associate itself with analycity at all. A standpoint which seems both more consistent with the way the semantic syllabus has been applied, and quite capable of coherent justification, is for it unashamedly to fly synthetic colours. It would then rally those who believe in synthetic methodology, who believe that synthetic teaching has created structurally competent students and who might predict that it can produce appropriate ones as well, as soon as we specify our teaching content in terms of categories of use. Certainly for many the solution to Newmark's problem which claims that the major step towards teaching "asking for a light" is taken when we accept "asking for a light" as an item we wish to teach cannot be dismissed out of hand. If semantic syllabuses do fly such colours, then we can recognise unequivocally what seems anyway to be the case, that there are indeed two general approaches to communicative language teaching which diverge—not because one is concerned with syllabus design and the other with methodology—but because each seems to carry different implications in terms of both syllabus design and methodology.

There is one sort of person for whom the conclusion that semantic syllabuses do not preclude a synthetic methodology is particularly important. It is the teacher who, disillusioned with the results of synthetic teaching, seeks salvation in the semantic syllabus. This sets him on a fresh analysis of language teaching content, this time made (initially) in semantic rather than structural terms. His discovery that the syllabus he eventually produces can (or has to?) be taught synthetically, will lead to further inevitable disillusionment.

Notes

1. This strategy is discussed at length in Paper 18. For other examples of "methodological approaches", see Allwright (1977), and Paper 12 of this volume.
2. The issues discussed in this and the following paragraph are highly relevant to the concerns of Paper 12.

Paper 11:

Use and Structure

One of the themes recurring throughout this volume is the relationship between structures and functions (and between the teaching of these two types of item). Paper 11 looks in detail at this question. Like the previous paper, it is theoretical. It argues that the lack of any obvious or close relationship between structures and functions makes the functional syllabus unsuitable as a vehicle for teaching grammar (the "strong claim" of Paper 11). Possible alternative approaches are then considered, one of them involving a new type of "communicative" syllabus. The theoretical justification for this syllabus is here discussed; more practical justifications are given in Paper 19, where the final section reintroduces the idea.

THE RELATIONSHIP between the teaching of use and structure has been a fraught one from the start. It is true that Wilkins (1976) and others have emphasised that whatever approach to language teaching is adopted, the teaching of structure remains a major objective. Yet the issue of whether structures can and should be taught through a functional syllabus has remained unresolved, and has become increasingly more urgent as teachers find that a communicative framework does not automatically lead to learning of the language system.[1] It is being felt more and more that, in Breen, Candlin and Waters' (1979) words: "our motive to provide learners with what seems to be a more meaningful frame of reference [i.e. through communicative/functional materials] has resulted, perhaps, in providing learners with a far *less* accessible and consistent framework than that provided by a pedagogic grammar."

Though authors rarely make explicit statements on the subject, currently available functional materials seem by implication or default to adopt one of two positions. In one (which we might for want of a better word call "separationist") the teaching of use through functional materials provides an added communicative dimension to the teaching. The implication is often of a two-stage overall strategy, with structure being taught first (through a structural syllabus) followed by a second communicative stage at which use is taught and where structures are "activated" or "recycled" in relation to functional categories. In some materials one finds a parallel rather than a sequential relationship, as for example, in Morrow and Johnson (1979) where structures and uses are both focused on, but in separate units. The position is "separationist" basically because it seems to imply a divorce between the teaching of forms and uses, though other kinds of related separation are often also being implied—as between knowledge and its "activation", between correctness and fluency. From the second, "unificationist", position the divorce of form and use is seen as undesirable and probably also untenable on linguistic and psycholinguistic grounds. The position argues for a communicative framework from the very beginning, and this framework is thus seen as providing an alternative teaching strategy rather than an "added dimension".[2]

The apparently central issue as to which of these opposing positions is more justifiable has been little discussed. In one of the few treatments of the problem Widdowson (1978b) considers two areas of current enquiry which have so far failed to come together—the American interlanguage studies and the British communicative/functional movement. The former, according to Widdowson, treat structure out of relation to use, while the latter concentrates on use and fails to link it in any meaningful way to structure. He says

> Although the importance of grammar may be acknowledged in principle in work such as that of van Ek (1975) and Wilkins (1976), this importance is seen essentially to reside in the fact that formal items are needed to expound conceptual and communicative categories; there is no suggestion that these categories are intrinsic to the system itself.

For the sake of exposition we might refer to the position Widdowson criticises in the quotation above as Standpoint 1. In it, structures are related to conceptual/communicative (Wilkins' semantico-grammatical/functional) categories in a list-like fashion without meaningful generalisations relating the two being made.[3] In terms of pedagogy this standpoint has been implemented through the grouping of structural items in relation to the conceptual/functional categories they expound. It is, in other words, the standpoint (by implication or default) behind present-day semantic syllabuses. From Widdowson's point of view this standpoint would presumably be considered well-nigh "separationist" by dint of being "failed unificationist".

Widdowson's objection to Standpoint 1 is a Hallidayean one. In Widdowson's terms "to describe communicative function in dissociation from the set of generative rules which realise it is to cut communication off from its cause and effect in system". In Halliday's terms: "The system of natural language can best be explained in the light of the social functions which language has evolved to serve" (Halliday (1970a) quoted by Widdowson).

Halliday's own attempts to link functional categories (like "scolding a child" in Halliday (1973)[4]) to the language system suggest a Standpoint 2 which, on the basis of his 1978 article, is Widdowson's. This standpoint claims not only that it *is* possible to relate functions and structures meaningfully but, further, that such relationships *must* be meaningfully made if we are to escape from the situation in which

> learners are being provided with language teaching programmes which attempt to develop communicative behaviour in dissociation from a knowledge of system and its meaning potential which can alone ensure that what is learned really is a capacity for communication, and not simply a collection of form/function correlates (Widdowson, 1978b, p. 10).

Widdowson does not discuss pedagogy in his paper, but nothing which he says there precludes adoption of a functional approach as long as this were to differ from present day functional approaches in the significant fact that it meaningfully related form and function. This then will be taken as at least one possible pedagogic implication of Standpoint 2.

Standpoint 2 is certainly a contentious one. Its validity is based on the belief not merely that systematic form/function relationships account for the way languages develop (cf. Halliday's statement that "language is as it is because of what it has to do"—Kress 1976, p. 17), but also that language learning proceeds through the perception of these relationships.[5] There is the further, underlying, belief that form/function relationships *can* be systematised, and this is not shared by Breen *et al.* (1979) who, interestingly also utilising Halliday, discuss the same issue.

For them, a network of systems (Halliday's textual, ideational and interpersonal) underlie "communicative knowledge", but these interrelate in an "inherently creative and potentially dynamic way". Thus what they call "data" (i.e. instances of language) result from the interrelationships between a set of underlying systems and are hence not accessible to systematisation. "Given", they say, "the present state of theory and research in language as *communication*, it seems that such data is *not* amenable to the kind of systematic organisation and categorisation which materials designers have been able to apply when presenting language as form."

We may call Breen *et al.*'s position Standpoint 3. It is, like Standpoint 1, not unificationist, because they are claiming that "the ongoing relationships *between* these three systems of knowledge [the textual, ideational, interpersonal] . . . cannot be reduced to some predictable or finite system of rules". But their position differs radically from Standpoint 1 in terms of pedagogic implication. They argue that since communication is not amenable to systematic organisation, prior selection and organisation of data (the function given to a syllabus) is meaningless. Thus unlike Standpoint 1 they make no attempt to list structures in relation to functions, and indeed appear more or less to advocate the abandonment of all selection and organisation even at beginner level. They advocate instead a "process approach" (in contradistinction to a "product approach" in which aspects of the language are itemised in the syllabus and presented discretely) whereby communicative abilities are developed through the learning process—students communicate about pieces of language as they learn about them. So Standpoint 3 is, unlike Standpoint 2, not unificationist; it differs from Standpoint 1 in that it makes no attempt to link structures and functions; and it is unlike both previous standpoints in that it abandons prior selection and organisation.[6]

It certainly seems sensible to acknowledge that the utility of any prior selection and organisation in teaching depends on our ability to point out meaningful relations and make a finite set of generalisations. Indeed, it is Standpoint 1's inability to do this that has led to the increasingly widespread discontent with communicative/functional materials noted earlier. The question of what meaningful relationships and generalisations can and cannot be made about language as communication is, therefore, crucial not merely to the question of syllabus design but (as Breen *et al.*'s methodological recommendations indicate) to all aspects of the teaching strategy.

Given that Breen *et al.* recognise a "system of systems" underlying "communicative knowledge", it is strange that they place so much emphasis on the unsystematisable nature of that knowledge. The underlying "system of systems" provides us surely with the generalisations we seek, with sets of knowledge which (because they are finite) can lead to meaningful preselection and hence syllabus design. A syllabus based on this "system of systems" would differ from the traditional structural type since it would link structures to meaning categories (and for this reason would be "communicative"). These categories might be much on the level of Wilkins' "semantico-grammatical", though if we opt to use Halliday we might classify in ideational, textual and interpersonal terms. It would then contain items like "being polite" (interpersonal), "distributing old and new information" or "emphasising (through cleft sentences) a point in the presence of a presupposed contradiction" (textual), and "past time reference" (ideational).[7]

To the extent that it might be called "semantico-grammatical" such a syllabus would not then differ radically from parts of Wilkins (1976). The important difference would lie in the fact that this would be no functional dimension—and the function is the category in Wilkins (1976) which has in fact been most used in practice as the basis of syllabus design. Indeed, it may well be that the problems considered in this paper have occurred simply because the function has held such a central position. The solution being discussed here would regard the function as an unhelpful level of analysis for language teaching purposes,[8] at which surface structures are linked according to pragmatic similarities but about which no valid grammatical generalisations can be, or (less contentiously) have as yet been, made. In Breen *et al.*'s terms the function would be seen as a label applicable at the level at which the underlying "system of systems" interrelates unsystematically in "communicative knowledge".

Once we admit the existence of finite systems, we have the basis for preselection and organisation through syllabus design, and this surely admits the feasibility of what Breen *et al.* call "product teaching". But for the reasons discussed in Breen *et al.* and touched on here, such a teaching would not account for the unsystematisable aspect of communication and would hence be incomplete. In other words, it does not provide the student with practice in interrelating the underlying "system of systems" to produce "data". The insight that this unsystematised element of communicative ability does exist sets the limits on the feasibility of pre-selected teaching (and hence syllabuses); in the same way that the systems underlying communicative knowledge set limits on the necessity for process type teaching. Both strategies are needed, to cater respectively for the systematised and the unsytematisable (or unsystematised).

This provides us, then, with a Standpoint 4. Unlike Standpoint 1 it makes no attempt to generalise in functional terms. Unlike Standpoint 2 it does not envisage doing so. Unlike Standpoint 3 it accepts a place for system and hence preselection in the teaching, at the same time recognising the necessity to practise the essentially dynamic and creative aspect of communication.

In practical terms it would entail a syllabus linking structures to interpersonal, textual and ideational categories. These categories would be taught discretely. The teaching would further involve communicative activities in which the student interrelated the "system of systems" to produce "data". The problem of linking these two types of teaching remains, but should not prove insuperable. Certainly one would wish to avoid a sequential treatment (with five years of systematic teaching followed by five years of communicative activity, for example).[9]

Notes

1. It may, of course, be too early to judge. We would certainly predict that the unsystematic presentation of structures which a truly functional syllabus implies would lead to a *slower* learning of structures. Lamentably, there has been no study of the comparative efficacy from this point of view of structural and functional syllabuses.
2. These two positions are discussed in relation to remedial teaching in Paper 9, and in theoretical terms in Paper 1, pages 21–2.
3. Wilkins' use of the label "semantico-grammatical" and his comments on the relationship between these categories and grammar in Wilkins (1973) make it clear that systematic relationships between *conceptual* and grammatical categories do hold. The same point is made in Paper 3 of this volume.
4. This attempt is described in detail in Paper 1.
5. This seems to be Halliday's position as expounded in Halliday (1970a).

6. Paper 19 in this volume argues along similar lines to Breen *et al.*, though it speaks of "combinatorial skill" rather than "communicative knowledge". Paper 12's approach involves the abandonment of prior linguistic selection and organisation.
7. A similar conclusion is reached in Paper 19 on the basis of experience in materials production. See page 212.
8. For *general* teaching purposes, that is. There may well be some teaching situations (e.g. certain short-term courses) where we opt to teach aspects of use without concern as to whether the student can make structural generalisations. See Paper 9.
9. The issues raised in this paper are amplified in Johnson (1980), which contains suggestions as to the ways in which the two types of teaching might be linked.

Paper 12:

The Procedural Syllabus

The previous paper considered various alternatives to the notional syllabus in a highly programmatic fashion. This paper looks in more depth at a further alternative—the "procedural" or "task-based" syllabus. It describes an experiment at present being conducted in Southern India using this type of syllabus. Then, in Part 2 of the paper, this syllabus type is discussed in relation to various versions of the notional syllabus. Because the procedural syllabus is "task" or "activity" based, many issues of methodology occur, and in this way the paper links with the following section.

THE AIM of this paper is to describe and discuss an experimental project at present being undertaken in Southern India. The project was begun in June 1979 by N. S. Prabhu (British Council English Study Officer in Madras) and the staff of the Regional Institute of English South India in Bangalore. It involves teaching a large class of thirteen-year-old pupils who had been learning English for three years when the project began.[1]

Part 1

Description of the Project

Prabhu's central hypothesis, which forms the basis of the project, is that "structure can best be learned when attention is focused on meaning". This is an explicit formulation of what many communicatively-orientated teachers practise (and of what is presumably the state of affairs in first language acquisition)—the primary focus of attention on performance of a task rather than on the language needed to perform it.[2]

There are for Prabhu two important consequences of this central hypothesis. The first involves the abolition of any kind of linguistic syllabus. He argues (Prabhu, forthcoming) that if we permit classroom language to be truly derived from the exigencies of some communicative task, then that language will not be systematic in any of the ways by which we usually systematise language (i.e. in structural, functional or notional terms). If, in other words, we truly let student and teacher say what they need and want to say in the performance of a communicative task, then their language will not follow any semantic or structural syllabus. Or, to state the issue the other way round, if we impose a semantic or structural syllabus on classroom language, we are taking away the teacher's and students' freedom to interact in a way natural to the task in hand.

Prabhu replaces the linguistic syllabus by what he calls a "procedural syllabus". This is a "syllabus of tasks" which are graded conceptually and grouped by similarity. The content of lessons is therefore planned in advance in terms of the task or activity it will involve, but no attempt is made to plan in terms of linguistic content.

The second consequence of the central hypothesis is to eschew any formal teaching procedures (such as drilling and error correction), where primary attention would be focused on "form" rather than "meaning". Details are discussed in the following section.

It is important to note that the procedural syllabus is not necessarily seen as the second stage of the kind of two-stage operation discussed in Paper 1.[3] The theory is *not* that the tasks the syllabus specifies will merely activate structures previously learned by traditional methods. The hypothesis is rather that through such activities the student will extend his repertoire; he will acquire language not previously known.

Details of the Project

The communicative activities which constitute the procedural syllabus include a variety of problem solving tasks involving map reading, the interpretation of timetables, solving simple whodunits, and so on.

Here is part of the syllabus at a stage where it is concerned with maps and plans (RIE, 1980).

43. Maps and plans—making the plan of a house (and labelling parts), following instructions; oral, then written, response
44. Maps and plans—task presented on paper
45. Maps and plans—charting movements from one part of the house to another; giving directions (e.g. "cross the living room, then turn right; go through the second door"); oral, then written, directions
46. Maps and plans—competition between groups (house plans supplied; each group demanding instructions from another)
47. Maps and plans—map of a few streets, with places marked; giving directions from one place to another; oral, then written, directions
48. Maps and plans—tasks presented on paper
49. Maps and plans—map of a district/state with different towns and roads marked; questions on possible routes from one town to another; oral, then written, responses
50. Maps and plans—map of a district/state, with distances indicated; choice of the shortest route and its distance; oral, then written, responses

51. Maps and plans—map of district/state, with roads and railway lines indicated; stating routes involving both rail and road (also, perhaps, places to be walked to); oral, then written, responses
52. Maps and plans—task presented on paper

Each lesson covers one task. This involves "a sustained period (say 15 minutes) of self-reliant effort by learners to achieve a clearly-perceived goal . . . . The effort involved should be an effort of the mind, and it should offer to learning a 'reasonable challenge'" (RIE, 1980). The remainder of the lesson is taken up by preparation for the task, plus, wherever possible, checking on its success. The question of mental effort is seen as crucial: "central to [the] methodology is the belief that when learners' minds are engaged in solving a problem . . . the resources that are needed for the purpose (both conceptual and linguistic) are best perceived and internalised" (RIE, 1980).

The teacher controls his classroom language in the same way that an adult controls language in conversation with a child. That is, he avoids items which will clearly be beyond his audience, and he freely glosses, rephrases, explains. Subject to such conditions, the teacher uses whatever language is necessary for execution of the task. According to the experimenters, following such guidelines "leads to an overall control in the teacher's language no lower than what one sees in 'structural' teaching though, being more natural, it is less perceptible" (RIE, 1980).

Various rules of thumb are suggested for the avoidance of language practice (where the primary focus of attention would be on "form" rather than "meaning").

> Occasional and explicit attention to language itself (e.g. "Do you know what X means? It means Y."; "This is the way to say it, not that."; "Be careful to spell this word correctly."; "Try to write neatly.") is legitimate, provided that: (1) it is incidental to—and seen by learners as necessary for—performing the task on hand; and (2) is done frankly and openly—as an adult does in talking to a child (or as a teacher of science or history does in teaching his subject), not as a hidden "moral" of some pretended activity or communication. Similarly, errors in learners' expression are to be treated by the teacher in the way a child's errors are treated by an adult, e.g. rephrased more accurately or corrected explicitly (not, however, elaborately, through a drill) or simply accepted provisionally as being adequate for the occasion—all as a form of temporary digression from (or clearing the way to) more important business, viz. the activity/task in hand (RIE, 1980).

A further interesting concept the project utilises is that of "incubation". The methodology eschews repetition practice through drilling, and the syllabus (because it avoids specification of linguistic items) is unlikely to lead to regular and paced coverage of such items. It is therefore unlikely that the students will hear and practise items in a systematic or intense way. The result may be a long period of "incubation" between the time that an item is first heard and its mastery by the student.

A second point needs to be made concerning exposure to the language. A potential criticism of the approach (partly discussed in RIE, 1980) is that in the absence of any structural or semantic planning, there is no way of ensuring adequate coverage of the language. It may happen that, because of the nature of the tasks selected, the student will continually be exposed to a restricted set of structural/semantic areas to the exclusion of other important areas. As regards structures, the criticism is convincingly met by the argument that, since the grammatical system is finite and generative, its main areas are certain to be covered (over a period of time) by any set of activities.[4] The situation regarding notions and functions is different. Since potentially useful notional/functional areas of a language are so large in number, it is doubtful whether the concept of "coverage" can be made to apply at all. The semantic syllabus attempts to identify particularly useful areas by a process of needs analysis, but because of the creative nature of communication, this process cannot lead to anything like coverage.[5]

The Project's Results[6]

For the first seven months the project encountered grave problems. Few pupils participated actively in the lessons, and the general reaction was one of bewilderment concerning the teacher's aims and methodology (reported in RIE, 1979). Matters slowly improved and towards the end of the year pupils were beginning to use structures which they had apparently not been taught in their previous years of English, and to which there is little likelihood of them having been exposed outside the classroom. The results of an evaluation test involving a control group are impressive, but the experimenters are cautious in their claims and are well aware of the evaluation problems associated with large-scale experimentation. More important perhaps than any formal evaluation is the experimenters' conviction that the approach is succceeding. The project is continuing into its second year.

Part 2

Discussion

In Paper 10 it was noted that what were there called "teaching content solutions" had little to say concerning methodology, while the "methodological solutions" remained uncommitted on questions of syllabus design. One of the attractions of the Bangalore project is its theoretical coherence; it adopts positions on both syllabus design and methodology, in each case derived from the one underlying hypothesis.

The (highly exploratory) discussion here will deal exclusively with syllabus design. It will consider two related respects in which the procedural syllabus might be felt to differ from other "communicative" syllabus types. It will conclude that the procedural syllabus does indeed differ from the "standard" (Wilkins, 1976) notional syllabus in these two respects, but that it is possible to conceive a "revised" notional syllabus in which this would not be the case.

The Terms of the Syllabus Specification

The procedural syllabus is stated in other-than-linguistic terms—in terms, that is, of tasks—and in a way which appears not to attempt a mapping out of linguistic content. For reasons which he discusses at length, Wilkins (1976) claims as an advantatge for the notional (as opposed to the structural) syllabus that it is, initially at least, made in behavioural (i.e. other-than-linguistic) terms. But (as noted in Paper 10) whatever the starting point, he clearly has the mapping out of linguistic content in mind and, in fact, states that "since it is language behaviour we are concerned with, it is possible, indeed desirable that the linguistic content of any unit [in notional teaching materials] should also be stated" (1976, p. 13).

For Wilkins the specification of linguistic content in a notional syllabus is, then, both possible and desirable. But is it inevitable? Procedural categories are non-linguistic ones, and if teaching based on these can indeed proceed without linguistic specification, then the same should hold true for notional categories which are likewise non-linguistic. It is certainly the case that many teachers and textbook writers (perhaps increasingly) regard functional materials as sets of communicative activities loosely linked by convenient functional labels, during the use of which little thought is given to precise language content. To the extent that the procedural syllabus can avoid linguistic specification, then, the notional syllabus should also be able to.

But to what extent can either syllabus type in fact achieve this? The point has already been made that the procedural syllabus grades tasks conceptually. Because Wilkins' "semantico-grammatical categories" are conceptual categories, the procedural syllabus is therefore open to the challenge that it is in fact a covert semantico-grammatical syllabus. The similarity between the two approaches becomes particularly apparent when considering the "rehearsal" or "sub-" tasks which the Bangalore project permits as preparation for the main tasks. In one map reading activity, for example, the pupils were found to have difficulty with concepts like "north-east" and "south-west". Sub-tasks were therefore introduced to teach the cardinal points—north, south, east and west. With tasks being broken down in this way, the resulting conceptual components are close to Wilkins' semantico-grammatical categories.

Given this similarity plus the fact that (following Wilkins' recommendations) notional syllabuses have in practice often involved linguistic specification, it is all the more relevant to ask whether the procedural syllabus can avoid the same "fate". Certainly sub-tasks of the type exemplified above are a species of pre-teaching, aiming to teach *something* which will be of utility in performance of the main task. They must therefore be based on some kind of specification of what the main task involves. But is the "something" stated in conceptual or linguistic terms? According to Prabhu (RIE, 1980), one of the aims of rehearsal is to ensure "that strategies for tackling the task (as well as the language that will be needed for the purpose) will, when needed, be available for recall and re-application". Some degree of linguistic preparation is therefore envisaged, and the language items involved constitute an (admittedly partial) linguistic specification of the tasks on the syllabus.

If there is indeed an (overt or covert) mapping out of language items, to what extent does this erode the project's basis? The answer will in practice depend on how much linguistic rehearsal is permitted. With pre-teaching of only a few essential items, teacher and pupils will maintain the freedom to interact in a way natural to the task at hand. With heavy pre-teaching this freedom will be lost and together with it the main motivation for using the task as the basis for syllabus design. Indeed, in the latter case it would be difficult to distinguish the approach from teaching based on a structural or notional syllabus, and where at the end of the lesson some communicative task involving taught structures or notions was given.

The degree of pre-teaching required will presumably suggest the extent to which linguistic mapping is desirable. If heavy pre-teaching becomes necessary it will be difficult to avoid the conclusion that pupils in the classroom simply cannot learn a language without concentration on discrete linguistic items which could then be stated in a syllabus (irrespective of whether it is derived from an initial specification of notions, function, tasks, or whatever).

To conclude this section: Paper 10 noted that the "methodological" solutions seemed to imply the abolition of the "linguistic" syllabus. This section has questioned whether the procedural syllabus can succeed in doing this any more than other syllabus types. If it can (and provided this characteristic is seen as desirable) then—the argument has been—a version of the notional syllabus different from the standard one might do the same.

The Status of the Syllabus Specification

The second (related) aspect of the procedural syllabus is that, recognising the impossibility of providing coverage of notional areas, it is a statement of "means" rather than a list of communicative "ends". The aim of the teaching is not performance of the tasks specified in the syllabus; these are the vehicle by which language is taught. The student is not, that is, learning map reading (the area of the syllabus exemplified earlier); he is learning English, through activities like map reading.

How does the notional syllabus stand in this respect? In Paper 9 a distinction is drawn between "weak" and "strong" claims for the notional (or, more specifically, the functional) syllabus. The weak claim sees it as an addition to, rather than a replacement of, the structural syllabus. Its specific aim is to provide competence in areas of use identified by needs analysis as being important to the students. The items appearing in the syllabus are therefore a specification of "ends". But according to the strong claim the notional syllabus is a replacement of the structural syllabus. The underlying belief is that the language system itself is best taught in relation to "uses", irrespective (the implication is) of whether the use categories one selects to teach the language system in relation to are ones which the student will ultimately need to perform. Thus our teaching materials might be made to include a unit on "Invitations" (for example), not necessarily out of a conviction that the student will ever need to invite in English, but in the belief that by being introduced to structures in relation to use categories (like *invitation*), the student will acquire language. In this formulation the notional syllabus, like the procedural syllabus, becomes a specification of means rather than ends; a set of "excuses to teach language" rather than a list of areas of use for which a need to be taught has been identified.

Conclusion

Part of the Bangalore project's interest for the European observer is that it provokes thought concerning the notional syllabus. It certainly comes at a time of questioning concerning the validity of the "standard" notional syllabus as a vehicle for teaching communication.[7] Discussion here has suggested that a "revised" version of the notional syllabus would be similar to the procedural syllabus in two important respects. It may even be true to say that more recent notional teaching has tended to move towards this "revised" position (and hence, in these important respects, towards the procedural syllabus). But of course the existence of a "revised" notional syllabus does not imply its superiority over a task-based alternative, and the relative merits of the two would need further consideration.

A final observation. It would certainly be a mistake to condemn the procedural syllabus on the basis of any lack of short-term results. The approach (with its built-in concept of "incubation") is likely to bear ill comparison in the short-term with more traditional approaches, where student reception and production is more evenly paced. It is nevertheless important that ultimate evaluation of the project should consider not only whether it works, but also whether it is the most cost-effective solution available. Many might predict success for the project in the long-term, but would wish to seek ways of speeding up the process. Because the project departs from traditional practice in so many ways (related to both syllabus design and methodology), there are rich possibilities for experimentation with the manipulation of variables. How would the project's methodology work when linked to a traditional syllabus (to the extent that this is feasible)? Would more traditional methods of error correction (for example) speed the learning process? Many such questions could be raised, and it is part of the project's value that it provides a framework in which they can be raised.[8]

Notes

1. I attended two seminars in Bangalore. The second, in April, 1980, was to monitor the project's progress at the end of its first year. The aim of the first (January, 1978) was to consider alternatives to the structural syllabus. During the course of this seminar, however, it became clear that the discontent which teachers in the region had been feeling for several years had its roots in methodology as much as syllabus design. The project avoids the kind of mistake noted in the final paragraph of Paper 10 by placing emphasis on changes in methodology. A number of people (including Widdowson, who attended a seminar in 1979) were directly or indirectly involved in the initiation of this project. But due acknowledgement must be given to Prabhu, and the first part of this paper merely reports on the stimulating work of him and his colleagues.
2. This idea is discussed in Paper 13, which speaks of a "task-orientated" language teaching.
3. See page 21.
4. Paper 8 develops this argument and notes that any structure which does not occur in a range of communicative activities is unlikely to be of central importance. These points are also made in RIE (1980).
5. This serious criticism of the notional/functional approach is mentioned in Paper 11. But see particularly the final section of Paper 19.
6. These cannot be reported in any detail here. See RIE (forthcoming) for a full report.
7. Papers 11 and 19 in particular highlight theoretical problems with the semantic syllabus.
8. See Johnson (1980) for further discussion of issues like these.

Section 4:

METHODOLOGY

Paper 13:

Some Communicative Processes

Most people have some intuitive idea of what the term "communicative" means when applied to methodology, and there are certainly common trends discernible in recent "communicative" materials. But if the approach is to develop coherently it must be based on clear ideas of what communicative processes various language activities involve. Paper 13 looks at this question specifically in relation to the skills of conversational interaction. But it is placed first in the section because most of the ideas discussed (particularly the concept of the "information gap") are relevant for the teaching of all language skills, in ways which are developed in later papers.

The paper is the second part of one entitled "Communicative approaches and communicative processes" *which appears in Brumfit and Johnson (1979).*

IN PAPER 10 the point was made that what was there called the "teaching content" approach to communicative language teaching bases itself on a linguistic insight regarding what is entailed in knowing a language, and that now, following Hymes, a revised view of language competence is generally accepted. Use of the word "knowing" in this context conjures up the spectre of a well-aired issue in applied linguistics—that "knowledge of a language" is not the same thing as "ability to use the language". It was often said of the grammar-translation method that it provided knowledge without skill, and a similar criticism can be levelled at our early attempts at communicative language teaching. If this is—as it surely is—a just criticism to level at any language teaching, then the implication is that methodologies should be based not only on insights

147

as to the nature of "knowledge of a language", but also on those concerned with the processes involved in its use. It is not a criticism that argues in favour of an analytic rather than a synthetic methodology[1] (though it may be one that applies most obviously to what Paper 10 calls the "teaching content solutions"). After all, the highly synthetic audio-lingual methodology certainly had a psychological base (even if it is one that we may now discredit). What it does argue in favour of is, simply, a methodology.

One of the aims of this paper is to suggest that communication science and skills psychology are two areas which can contribute considerably (and in a way as yet only partially exploited) to the development of a communicative methodology. Specifically, we shall here consider some processes relevant to the teaching (and testing) of speaking. To provide a basis for discussion, consider the following set of possible simple interactions:

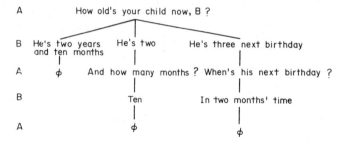

In this situation A's aim is to find out B's child's age in years and months. In order to do this he asks the question, "How old's your child now, B?" A number of possible interactional sequences might follow. In one, B replies, "He's two years and ten months." A compares this piece of information with the information he requires. He finds the two match, and the interaction therefore ends. In a second possible interaction, B replies, "He's two." When A compares this information with the required information, he finds a discrepancy. He now knows the child's age in years, but not in months. His next question—"And how many months?" —is calculated to eliminate this discrepancy. He is given the reply "Ten.", and the interaction ends. In a third possible interaction, B replies,

"He's three next birthday." After comparing given information with required information, A formulates the question, "When's his birthday?" B's reply eliminates the mismatch between given and required, and the third interaction closes.

There are at least three processes which A must undertake if he is to fulful his role as interactant. Firstly, he must "scan" B's utterance to extract what Cherry (1957) calls its "pragmatic information". Pragmatic information is not equivalent to semantic information; it is that part of the total information conveyed which contributes to the information required by the speaker. It is, in short, information which the listener wants to receive. In order to receive this information the listener must maintain a state of readiness. He approaches the task of listening comprehension prepared to search for certain pieces of information in his interactant's words. Once this information comes, it has to be assessed according to the speaker's aim, and this is the second process which A must undertake. The process is, in Mackay's (1972), one of "evaluation whereby some indication of the current outcome is compared against some internal 'target criterion' [what we have called 'speaker aim'] so that certain kinds of discrepancy or 'mismatch' would evoke activity calculated to reduce that discrepancy." A compares, then, what he is told with what he wants to know, identifies any mismatch and then—as a third process—formulates his next utterance. This he does by selecting from what Halliday (1970b, p. 142) calls the "large number of interrelated options" embodied in the "meaning potential". The three interactions considered earlier in the "asking how old the child is" situation constitute only a small part of the total possible number which the interactants could have followed; just as Halliday's ways of scolding a child (see Paper 1 in this volume) represent only a small number of the possible ways of expounding that function.

If interactions are to continue in a natural way, the formulation of utterances and the processes of scanning and evaluation which precede it must of course be made extremely quickly—within "real time". The ability to do this is what we generally mean by fluency in a language. The teaching of fluency (an objective which has tended to be ignored in the past) thus needs consciously to involve practice in these processes.

The first, most central, and by now most generally accepted, implication of the nature of these processes is that they can only really be practised in a language teaching which is "task-orientated".[2] We are now accustomed to the view of language as a tool developed to serve us in Halliday's social contexts and behavioural settings. We also now recognise that past language teaching often failed to practise language to some purpose, focusing attention on "how" without providing a "why". One way in which such a language teaching fails is that it does not develop fluency in the processes involved in language use. We cannot expect listeners to approach interactions in a state of readiness, to learn how to scan for pragmatic information, unless we provide them with a reason for scanning; nor can we expect them to evaluate incoming information against a speaker aim, unless we provide them with a speaker aim (a communicative intent). Finally we cannot expect them to make appropriate selection from meaning potential unless they have an intention from which to derive meaning. This point is well exemplified by an anecdote from Savignon (1972) who uses role play techniques to practise greetings in French with a group of students. The first volunteer walks up to the female experimenter and says, "Bonjour, monsieur." Everyone realises, in Savignon's words, "how much they needed practice in linking expression to actual meaning". There is indeed a crucial difference between practice involving the linking of expression to actual meaning, where expression is made to serve actual meaning—and practice in which the student's attention is focused on achieving correctness of expression. The difference doubtless partially accounts for Krashen's (1976) two systems for second language performance.[3]

It is for reasons such as this that fluency in communicative process can only develop with a "task-orientated teaching"—one which provides "actual meaning" by focusing on tasks to be mediated through language, and where success or failure is seen to be judged in terms of whether or not these tasks are performed.

A second implication relating to these processes concerns the concept of information. "Conveying information" and "communicating" are similar, though not identical notions. In a large number of conversational interactions the purpose of communicating is to convey information—factual information, information concerning feelings, information about what we wish to be done. The concept of conveying information involves, as many linguists have testified, a notion of doubt. We can only be said to be conveying a piece of information to someone if they do not already know it. As Lyons (1968, p. 413) says, "if the hearer knows in advance that the speaker will inevitably produce a particular utterance in a particular context, then it is obvious that the utterance will give him no information when it occurs; no 'communication' will take place". "Information" in Cherry's (1957, p. 168) words this time, "can be received only when there is doubt."

It is the absence of this element of doubt in much language teaching which makes it non-communicative. The conventional techniques of "commentary" (telling a story from pictures, retelling it after the teacher, describing actions taking place in the classroom) provide useful structural practice but do not involve communication. Such practice fails in two ways. Firstly it does not generally capture student interest, and this may well be a significant factor contributing to the unpopularity of foreign languages in school curricula—one recipe for boredom being the repetition of the known to the knowers.

But equally importantly it fails to involve the processes by which interaction takes place. These processes depend crucially on the existence of an information gap. If the listener already knows the pragmatic information content of what his interactant will say, then no scanning for such content will take place; nor will responses be formulated within real time based on information just received. In this sense the existence of doubt is a vital prerequisite to fluency practice.

The attempt to create information gaps in the classroom, thereby producing communication viewed as the bridging of the information gap, has characterised much recent communicative methodology. These attempts take many forms. Wright (1976) achieves it by showing out-of-focus slides which the students attempt to identify. Byrne (1978) provides incomplete plans and diagrams which students have to complete by asking for information. Allwright (1977) places a screen between students and gets one to place objects in a certain pattern; this pattern is then communicated to the student behind the screen. Geddes and Sturtridge (1979) develop "jig-saw" listening in which students listen to different taped materials and then communicate their contents to others in the class. Most of these techniques operate by providing information to some and withholding it from others. Often it is the students who give information to each other, but sometimes—particularly when the language is to be learned receptively rather than productively—it is more appropriate for the teacher to play this role. Morrow and Johnson (1979), for example, ask students to follow street directions given by the teacher and to mark given locations on a map. In this exercise, it is the receptive understanding of directions rather than the production of them which is being practised.

Providing information to some and withholding it from others is one of several ways to create an information gap. Another, which constitutes the final aspect of communication to be considered here, is simply to permit the student some choice in what he says.

The concepts of selection and doubt are closely linked. To continue the earlier quotation from Cherry, "information can be received only when there is doubt; and doubt implies the existence of alternatives—where choice, selection or discrimination is called for". If Speaker A can select what he says, then Listener B will be in doubt as to what will be said to him; speaker selection implies listener doubt. Thus if we create classroom situations in which the students are free to choose what to say, the essential information gap will have been created.

But the importance of selection goes far beyond its utility in the creation of information gaps. Central to Halliday's view of language (partially exemplified in Paper 1 of this volume) is that it constitutes sets of options at various levels. The *concept* of selection, as choice from various sets of options, is thus basic to the concept of communication; and the *process* of selection in real time from various sets of options is basic to the process of fluent communication. From this point of view communicative language teaching may be seen as the provision to students of sets of options from which selection can be made. It must also provide practice in the process of selecting from these options within real time.

One of the major advantages (one might indeed argue *the* major advantage) of teaching materials that are organised functionally or according to some other non-structural principle, is that they provide the opportunity to present language in semantically-homogeneous units. This makes it possible to practise interactions which (like "real" interactions) centre upon related semantic areas; also, to practise the process of selection from a semantic network in real time. Thus when we teach "invitations", for example, we can deal not only with inviting, but with accepting and declining invitations as well, giving a number of alternative exponents for each. What we are providing is a set of semantic options for the network of invitations. Once this is provided, we can practise selection from it in real time: Student A can invite (selecting from the various exponents provided), and Student B can select whether to accept or decline (again choosing from various exponents, at the same time making sure that his exponent is textually appropriate to the exponent of invitation he hears). It will be the materials producer's task to provide techniques by which this process of selection can be meaningfully made (i.e. in relation to a created context).[4]

As the students work through the materials, and as long as the syllabus has been constructed to deal with interactionally-related semantic areas in sequence,[5] the selections which we can expect the student to make will increase exponentially. Consider for example a possible situation in which we follow our "Invitations" unit with one on "Making Arrangements". The number of interaction sequences involving selection might be as follows:

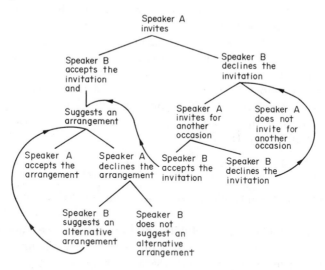

In a structural syllabus the situation is different. Language is presented in structurally-homogeneous but semantically-heterogeneous units, the result being that semantically-related but structurally-unrelated sequences (for example "invitation–acceptance" where the exponents used are structurally unrelated) will tend not to occur. This is partly because in their desire to focus on structural concerns the materials will actively seek structurally-homogeneous interactions, and partly because the structural grading will at any given point restrict the number of semantically-related interactions the student can handle. Consequently most of the communicative practice in which the students will have to develop interactions involving the selection of realistic options from a semantic network will tend to occur towards the end of a structural course, when the students' structural knowledge is developed. Certainly such practice, important to the development of fluency, will not occur regularly throughout the course.

This paper has considered ways in which classroom teaching procedures can be made to reflect a coherent model of communicative skill. Similar remarks may be made about testing procedures. It is certainly the case that testing (as teaching) must be concerned not only with "knowledge of a language" but also with "ability to use it". We must do more, that is, than ask the student whether he *knows* that Exponent X is appropriate to Intent Y in Context Z; we must find out whether he *is able to produce* Exponent X when he intends Y in context Z.

It may be that a valuable and insufficiently tapped source of inspiration for the testing of fluency of communicative process lies in the area of skills psychology. Reed (1968), for example, lists a number of ways in which skilled performance differs from non-skilled performance, and his observations on the variable of speed are particularly relevant to the question of fluency. He says,

> In many skilled activities improvement is assessed in terms of speed and it is commonly assumed that the overall time taken to complete any activity reflects the level of skill. But in absolute terms this is not necessarily so . . . . As Woodworth (1938) pointed out, expert performance is not merely that of the beginner executed more quickly.

Other important indicators of skilled performance are: the "suppression of flourishes"; the ability to carry out a task with less information; confidence; the ability to check mistakes; anticipation; automation; reliability. The extent to which these various measures can be related to language teaching through formal testing procedures is of course doubtful, but at least some (the ability to carry out a task with less information; the ability to check mistakes; anticipation) might be explored. It is particularly interesting to note that the ability to recognise and check one's own mistakes is, according to Bartlett (1947) "the best single measure of mental skill."[6]

Notes

1. See Paper 10 for discussion of these terms.
2. Prabhu (see Paper 12) uses the concept of "task orientation" as the basis for his approach.
3. The concept of "meaningful language practice" (e.g. in Dakin, 1973) as practice involving relating language to a situation is, of course, generally accepted. What is intended here is something more, in which the language is not merely related to a situation but "made subservient" to it. This is the case, for example, in the proposals discussed in Paper 12.
4. This may be done, for example, by providing realia, such as a diary in which the student fills in appointments. He then accepts invitations at times when he is free and declines them when he is not. This is the technique used in Johnson and Morrow (1979) and in other materials.
5. By application, that is, of the criterion of "sequencing potential" discussed in Paper 5.
6. Cloze procedures do, of course, test anticipation.

Paper 14:

Making Drills Communicative

In Paper 8 the possibility of a "communicative structural" approach was discussed. Some suggestion of how such an approach might be realised is now given here. Paper 14 asks whether there can be such a thing as a communicative drill, and concludes that there can. It provides an example of a communicative drill, and thereby illustrates in a concrete way two of the principles discussed more theoretically in Paper 13. One is the principle of the information gap; the other is what this paper calls the principle of "getting the student to utilise in some way information given in the course of an exercise". This second principle relates to the concept, discussed in Paper 13, of a "task-orientated" language teaching.

This paper was published in Modern English Teacher, 7, 4, 1980.

WHEN we think of "communicative" language practice our thoughts turn perhaps most naturally to exercises (like role play) associated with the free production stage. In fact we may even be tempted to equate the idea of "being communicative" with the notion of "letting the student say what he wants to say", implying a minimum of control. At the same time most of us—however "communicative" we are in our approach—would accept the need for controlled practice or "drilling"; but we tend to think of these two things—"communicative practice" on the one hand and "drilling" on the other—as being quite separate. We provide both, but in different parts of the lesson. This short paper explores the concept of the "communicative drill", and suggests that by following quite simple procedures we may change traditional drills into more communicative ones.

We are all familiar with the following kind of traditional drill[1]:

Ask:

Is	Janet Tom Peter Alan Jillian	standing sitting	by the window? on the stairs? by the door? on the bus? on the scooter?

Answer:

Yes,	he	is
No,	she	isn't

Exercise 1

Here the students may work in pairs with Student A asking and Student B answering. The drill will produce exchanges like this:

A: Is Peter sitting by the window?
B: Yes, he is.

A: Is Janet standing on the stairs?
B: No, she isn't.

Here is another exercise. It uses the same pictures, but there the similarity ends:

A.

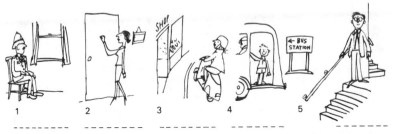

Ask your partner a question, and write names under the pictures.

	standing	by the window? on the stairs? by the door?
Who's that		
	sitting	on the bus? on the scooter?

B. Give your partner information

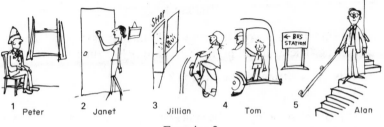

Exercise 2

Students work in pairs. Student A covers the bottom part of the drill with a piece of blank paper, and student B covers the top part. A asks questions like "Who's that standing on the bus?", "Who's that sitting by the window?" B supplies the names, which A must write under the picture. When the exercise is done, A checks his answers either by looking at B's part of the page or by asking questions such as "It's Peter sitting by the window, isn't it?"

Exercise 2 is in certain respects more "communicative" than Exercise 1. In fact a rather detailed comparison of the two exercises will involve a useful exploration of what it is that makes a language teaching exercise "communicative" or otherwise. Some points of comparison.

1. The information gap principle has already been discussed in Paper 13. In Exercise 1 both students are looking at the same page; so Student A is asking questions to which he already knows the answers, and Student B is supplying answers which he knows A already has. However useful the drill may be as structural practice, it is, from this communicative point of view, a charade. No information is changing hands. Exercise 2 remedies this by asking the students to look at different parts of the page and by supplying one picture without names. It provides, in other words, information to some students which it withholds from others; so B does not know what A will ask[2] and A does not know how B will reply. There is an information gap, and hence communication viewed as a "bridging of the information gap".

In Paper 13 it was noted that the information gap is important to ensure practice of the processes of communication. This can be illustrated even in the highly restricted context of the two drills. Consider Student A's role in Exercise 1. There is no reason at all why he should listen to or process what is said to him. He already knows the answer to the questions he is asking. In fact, he could very well block his ears while B is replying. The drill would proceed without problems.

2. In Exercise 2 there is an information gap. But notice that this is not in itself enough to make Student A listen and process. It is a necessary but not a sufficient condition. Imagine for a moment that we did not ask A to write down the names of the characters. He would still be able to block his ears while B replied—not as in the case of Exercise 1 because there is no information gap, but simply because he would have no *reason*

to listen. He is not being asked to *do anything* with the information he is being given; hence he has no motivation for listening and processing. It is the words "write names under the pictures" which ensure that his ears must be unblocked—that he will listen and process. These words make Exercise 2 conform to a principle important in communicative language teaching—the principle of "getting the student to utilise in some way information given in the course of an exercise." Here the utilisation is the simple and rather mechanical one of writing down names; but in more extended exercises it will involve more meaningful activities such as reporting received information to other members of the class, using it to write a letter or fill in a questionnaire, and so on.

3. There is a difference in the language that the two exercises practise. One group of teachers was asked to imagine a situation in which the sentence "Is Peter sitting by the window?" might be used. After much deliberation the group arrived at a situation in which a group of ambushers was waiting inside a house for its victim. Their leader was checking they were all in position. Hardly an everyday situation! The same group of teachers had no trouble in imagining a context for "Who's that sitting by the window?" It might be said, for example, at a party by someone who does not know the names of many guests. The sentences generated by Exercise 2 are thus, as they stand, likely to be more "useful" to the student.

We might formulate this by predicting that the function of "asking about the identity of a person" (as in Exercise 2) is likely to be more useful to the student than the function of "checking the location of a person" (as it is demonstrated in Exercise 1). But the danger with Exercise 1 is greater than this formulation suggests, as is revealed if we ask ourselves exactly how the student will react to this exercise. One possibility is that—given the way the practice situation is set up, with various named characters in various locations—the student will see the task as one of *asking about identity* rather than *checking location*. He will then come away with the idea that one way of *asking about identity* in English is to use a sentence like "Is Peter sitting by the window?" This is perhaps a rather far-fetched possibility in the given situation, but there are other occasions where it may well happen. Here is one exchange found in a textbook dialogue:

A: When does the train go to X?
B: Every half hour, and on Sundays every two hours.

If most native speakers were asked this question they would probably interpret it as a *request for information about the departure of the next train,* and would reply "at 9.30." or "In ten minutes time." But B interprets it as a *request for information about the frequency of trains.* Having practised this dialogue the student can be forgiven for interpreting it in the same way and for using it like this outside the classroom.

More likely in the case of Exercise 1, though, is that the student will in fact interpret "Is Peter sitting by the window?" as a question *checking location.* But he will also realise how unnatural it is to ask questions like this in the situations as set up. His perception of the artificiality of the exercise will make him feel that he is "doing a language drill' rather than "using the language to do something". The student doing Exercise 1 can hardly see it as other than a language teaching exercise. It is, in Widdowson's (1978a) terms, practice in "usage" rather than "use".[3]

Getting the student to use language in inappropriate practice situations thus has two dangers. It either leads to inappropriate use of language outside the classroom, or it results in a sterile kind of practice in which language is viewed as a "system of rules" rather than as a "means of communicating messages".

A final point about language. We tend perhaps to feel that as soon as we try to "be communicative" in the classroom, language content becomes more complex. We might in fact be tempted to use these two exercises as an example of this, pointing out that the present continuous interrogative in Exercise 1 is structurally simpler than the "Who's that sitting ... ?" structure in Exercise 2. But it is not true to say that "communicative" implies "complex". It may be true that a sentence like "Is Peter sitting by the window?" will occur rarely outside the classroom; but it is certainly *not* true that the present continuous interrogative as a structure is rare or communicatively unuseful. And precisely because the structure is common, it is easy to find practice situations in which it will be naturally used. Sentences like, for example, "Is Peter going to the cinema tonight?" are in everyday use and can be practised through drills using perhaps a table which tells the students what various characters plan to do one evening. Simple structures as well as complex ones have communicative currency, and as long as the initial question is "in what situations is this structure commonly used?", there is no reason why simple structures should not be practised in a natural way.

The discussion has indicated three ways in which we may call Exercise 2 "communicative". It involves, firstly, an information gap; secondly, the student is asked to "utilise" information given in the course of the exercise—he must write the names down. Thirdly, the language generated by the drill is natural to the practice situation and is likely to be useful to the student outside the classroom. Nor is it a particularly difficult task to construct drills of this type. With a small amount of work the teacher who is forced to use a traditional textbook can make his teaching more communicative by modifying the drills along the lines suggested above.

Notice finally that however "communicative" Exercise 2 may be, it remains a drill. It has the central characteristic of drills—that it involves repetition of a restricted area of the language system. The purpose of the exercise is to practise one structure ("who's that" + "-ing") a good many times in a short space of time.

This fact leads towards an interesting conclusion. Because it involves repetition of one structure, Exercise 2 could be used in a structurally (as opposed to a functionally) organised course, in the unit dealing with that grammar point. Therefore if we accept that the exercise is communicative, this surely implies that a structurally organised course may be communicative—at least in the senses discussed above. There is a tendency to assume today that being communicative automatically involves being functional. But there seems little reason why one cannot practice important communicative processes within a structural syllabus.[4]

Notes

1. The pictures are taken from *Success with English*, G. Broughton, Penguin, 1968, but the drill is a very substantial adaptation of the original.
2. This much is true in Exercise 1 also.
3. In the terms used in Paper 13 it focuses attention on "how" without providing a "why".
4. This point was also central to the argument developed in Paper 8, and Exercise 2 here illustrates how the kind of approach discussed in Paper 8 might be realised.

Paper 15:

Five Principles in a "Communicative" Exercise Type

The starting point for this paper is an exercise type which demonstrates five important principles. Some of these principles have been discussed before in previous papers, but the context here is a different one. For example, in Paper 14 the "getting the student to utilise information" principle is discussed in relation to the receptive skills. It here becomes the "task dependency" principle, and the emphasis is now on its importance for the teaching of language production. The example of the exercise type which is used as the basis for discussion is relevant to the teaching of advanced writing; but the point is made that the exercise type itself is highly productive and can be used at various levels, for the teaching of various skills. The paper contains several further examples which illustrate this.

Paper 15 has not appeared elsewhere, though it draws heavily from the writer's contribution to Johnson and Morrow (1981) dealing with the teaching of writing.

Introduction

THE FOLLOWING are the student instructions for an exercise occurring in a unit on "Describing Objects."[1]

> Many inventions were made in the Ancient World. Work in pairs. Student A looks at the diagram of an Egyptian invention on page 107. Student B looks at the diagram of a Greek machine on page 105. Each write a description. Then show your description to your partner, who must try to draw a diagram of it. If his diagram is wrong, make your description clearer, so that the diagram is correct.

This exercise, which for ease of reference will be called the Greek Machine exercise, is intended for advanced students. But it exemplifies a highly productive sequence which may be used at a variety of levels:

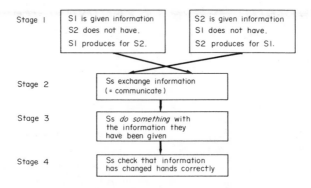

This paper will consider five principles embodied in this sequence, illustrating where appropriate with further examples.

1. The Information Transfer Principle

A central characteristic of communicative language teaching is that it focuses attention on the ability to understand and convey information content. One way to practise (and test) these abilities is through information transfer exercises. The following reading comprehension exercise is "communicative" to the extent that the student is being asked, not to comment on any point of grammatical structure or lexical meaning, but to extract certain pieces of information and to transfer them onto the application forms.[2]

Example 1

In Winton there is a very good sports club which welcomes applications from overseas visitors.

Look at these two letters. They contain information about two people who want to join the club. Fill in application forms for these people below.

```
                        29, Gosforth Close,
                        Hamford,
                         Nottingham,
                          Notts.
                           NG16 7EA

                        1 Feb. 1979
Dear John,

    I don't know whether you remember
me - we met very briefly at Michael
Everton's party last week.  My name is
Arturo Catania and I'm an Italian
doctor. My wife told me after the
party that you're the secretary of the
sports club, which I'm very interested
in joining.  Could you please send me
some information about how to apply.
If you wish to phone me for any reason,
my number's Hamford (0273) 51469.

            Yours sincerely,

            Arturo Catania

            Arturo Catania
```

```
                        2b, Lakeside Avenue,
                        Upton,
                        Notts. NG16 7AA

                        13 Jan. 1979

Dear Sir,
    I wish to become a member of the Winton
sports club, and would be grateful to receive
details of subscription rates and other
relevant information.  I am a teacher by
profession, and shall be in England for 2 years
(my nationality is French).  I was born in
Paris on the 12th of January 1939.
    I look forward to hearing from you.

            Yours faithfully,

            Odette Marie François

            (Miss) Odette Marie Francois
```

```
WINTON SPORTS CLUB: MEMBERSHIP APPLICATION

Surname  CATANIA      First Name(s) _____

Date of Birth  4.8.46   Nationality _____ Marital Status ___

Address _____

Telephone Number _____  Occupation _____
```

```
WINTON SPORTS CLUB: MEMBERSHIP APPLICATION

Surname _____  First Name(s)  Odette Marie _____

Date of Birth _____  Nationality _____ Marital Status ___

Address _____

Telephone Number _____  Occupation _____
```

A similar principle may be used for practising listening comprehension, with the initial information given through taped dialogues. Thus in Example 1 the information about Arturo and Odette might be given through dialogues which they have with the Winton Sports Club secretary.

In the same way that communicative reading and listening practice is concerned with the *understanding* of information content, communicative writing and speaking practice should deal with the productive equivalent of this ability: the *conveying* of information content. Information transfer exercises may be used here also. Stage 1 of the Greek Machine exercise involves transfer of information from diagram to descriptive passage. Similarly, a productive equivalent of Example 1 could be devised by providing the student with a completed application form and asking him either to write the original letter of application or to role play the dialogue between applicant and Club Secretary. The first of these alternatives is given below:

Example 2

In Winton there is a very good sports club which welcomes applications from overseas visitors.

Arturo Catania applied to join this club. He wrote a letter to the Club Secretary who used it to fill out an application form for Arturo. Here is the form. Use it to write Arturo's letter of application.

```
WINTON SPORTS CLUB: MEMBERSHIP APPLICATION

Surname  CATANIA        First Name(s)  Arturo

Date of Birth  4·8·46   Nationality  Italian   Marital Status  M

Address  29, Gosfirth Close, Hamford, Nottingham NG16 7EA

Telephone Number  (0273)51469   Occupation  Doctor.
```

Example 1 involves information transfer from letter to application form, Example 2 from application form to letter, and the Greek Machine exercise from diagram to written passage. Other variations of this principle might entail transfer (for example) from map to passage or vice versa; passage or tape to table or graph, and so on.

2. The Information Gap Principle

We cannot really claim that Examples 1 and 2 truly involve *conveying* information. There is certainly information *transfer*, but transferring and conveying are not quite the same thing. The former, as interpreted here, involves a transmission of "medium" (from letter to application form, for example) while the transmission in the latter is from person to person. Central to the concept of conveying is the idea of the "naive receiver"—a person who does not initially possess the information and who receives it by means of the spoken or written communication. In the Greek Machine exercise this occurs at Stage 2 and the communication is signified by the crossing lines joining Stages 1 and 2.

The information gap principle, which makes this conveying of information possible, has already been discussed in this volume with particular reference to the speaking skill.[3] One reason why the principle is useful for the teaching of speaking is that it creates a condition of unexpectedness; with Student 2 not knowing in advance what Student 1 will say, the former must formulate his responses quickly, thereby developing fluency. Because writing does not involve rapid exchanges with another person this element of the unexpected is less crucial. But there are two other reasons why the information gap principle is important for the teaching of writing, as for speaking. Firstly, because it permits genuine information flow in the class; the students tell each other things they do not already know. Secondly (and as a consequence of the first reason), the condition is created whereby the assessment of written or spoken work can focus attention on whether it succeeds in "getting the message across". This occurs at Stages 3 and 4 of the Greek Machine exercise where the student's written work is utilised by his partner and is assessed on its adequacy for the production of an accurate diagram. This point is developed below under Principle 5.

3. The Jigsaw Principle[4]

Here is a version of Example 2 involving an information gap.

Example 3

Student 1

In Winton there is a very good sports club which welcomes applications from overseas visitors.

i) Arturo Catania applied to join this club. He wrote a letter to the Club Secretary who used it to fill out an application form for Arturo. Here is the form. Use it to write Arturo's letter of application.

```
WINTON SPORTS CLUB: MEMBERSHIP APPLICATION

Surname   CATANIA        First Name(s)  Arturo

Date of Birth  4·8·46    Nationality  Italian   Marital Status  M

Address  29, Gosfirth Close, Hamford, Nottingham  NG16 7EA

Telephone Number  (0273)51469   Occupation  Doctor.
```

- -

Student 2

In Winton there is a very good sports club which welcomes applications from overseas visitors. Your partner has written a letter of application from someone to join the club. Use this letter to fill in the application form.

```
WINTON SPORTS CLUB: MEMBERSHIP APPLICATION

Surname _____   First Name(s) _____

Date of Birth _____   Nationality _____  Marital Status ___

Address _____

Telephone Number _____   Occupation _____
```

Here Student 1 is the producer (practising writing) and Student 2 the receiver (practising reading comprehension). To ensure that both students practise both skills we may follow the exercise with a second in which the students' roles are reversed—Student 2 writes and Student 1 reads. The jig-saw principle streamlines the operation by getting both students to write at the same time. In the Greek Machine exercise Student 2 writes for Student 1 at the same time as Student 1 is writing for Student 2. They then exchange information to complete the "jig-saw". On the following page is an expanded version of Example 3 which uses this principle and hence follows a sequence identical to the Greek Machine exercise.

Example 4

Student 1

In Winton there is a very good sports club which welcomes applications from overseas visitors.

i) Arturo Catania applied to join this club. He wrote a letter to the Club Secretary who used it to fill out an application form for Arturo. Here is the form. Use it to write Arturo's letter of application.

```
WINTON SPORTS CLUB: MEMBERSHIP APPLICATION

Surname  CATANIA          First Name(s)  Arturo

Date of Birth  4·8·46    Nationality  Italian   Marital Status  M

Address  29, Gosfirth Close, Hamford, Nottingham NG16 7EA

Telephone Number  (0273) 514 69   Occupation  Doctor.
```

ii) Your partner has written a letter of application from another person. Use this letter to fill in the application form from that person.

```
WINTON SPORTS CLUB: MEMBERSHIP APPLICATION

Surname _____    First Name(s) _____

Date of Birth _____    Nationality _____  Marital Status ___

Address _____

Telephone Number _____    Occupation _____
```

Student 2

In Winton there is a very good sports club which welcomes applications from overseas visitors.

i) Odette François applied to join this club. She wrote a letter to the club who used it to fill out an application form for Odette. Here is the form. Use it to write Odette's letter of application.

```
WINTON SPORTS CLUB: MEMBERSHIP APPLICATION

Surname  FRANCOIS        First Name(s)  Odette Marie

Date of Birth  12/1/39   Nationality  French   Marital Status  S

Address  26, Lakeside Avenue, Upton, Notts, NG 16 7AA

Telephone Number  (0273) 63159   Occupation  Teacher
```

ii) Your partner has written a letter of application from another person.
Use this letter to fill in the application form from that person.

```
WINTON SPORTS CLUB: MEMBERSHIP APPLICATION

Surname _____   First Name(s) _____

Date of Birth _____   Nationality _____  Marital Status ___

Address _____

Telephone Number _____   Occupation _____
```

4. The Task Dependency Principle

In Paper 14 mention was made of the principle whereby the student is
asked "to utilise in some way information given in the course of an
exercise". This may be called the "task dependency principle". According
to it, we create wherever possible a Task 2 which can only be done if a
Task 1 has been successfully completed. In the Paper 14 example the
Task 2 simply involved writing down names, but in the Greek Machine
exercise the task is far more considerable; the student utilises his
partner's description (the Task 1) to draw a diagram (the Task 2).

As noted in Paper 14, the principle is important for the teaching of
receptive skills simply to ensure that the listening or reading gets done;
without a *reason* for listening or reading, the student will probably fail to
do either. But the principle is also relevant to the productive skills
because it helps to foster in the student an "accountability" for the way he
uses language. A difference between classroom and real world which can
never be eradicated is that the former shields the student from the

consequences of his mistakes. Street directions given wrongly in the classroom lead only to teacher correction; in the real world they result in someone getting lost. Task dependencies can help to minimise this difference; the student's knowledge that someone in the class will read his letter and utilise its information content (returning with a complaint if that content is inadequate) will affect the way he tackles his task. Similarly, the student writing in the Greek Machine exercises knows that he is accountable to his partner and that his description will be assessed on its adequacy for the production of a diagram.

5. The Correction for Content Principle

The points in the preceding paragraph lead on to the final principle to be discussed here. As already noted under Principle 1, communicative *practice* of the productive skills should deal with the conveying of information. Similarly, the communicative *correction* of the productive skills should assess whether information content has been correctly conveyed. The Greek Machine exercise is designed with this in mind. The students are writing *for each other* knowing that their written work will not be assessed in the first instance by the teacher for its grammatical correctness but by their partner for its adequacy in the production of a diagram. That is (in Widdowson's (1978a) terms) it is initially being regarded as a specimen of "use" rather than "usage".

For this reason Stage 4 is particularly important, as is also the condition that if the produced diagram is inadequate this should lead to revision of the written work. With the task set up in this way the students receive feedback on the communicative efficacy of their written work.

The correction for content principle argues that *at some stage* the student's language production should be judged on its communicative efficacy in relation to a specific task. But the principle does not negate the utility of teacher correction for grammatical accuracy *at some other stage*. Language is a system developed for communicative purposes. It has evolved means of expressing distinctions because those distinctions are there to express. In Halliday's (1970a) words, "language is as it is because of what it has to do". The student with imperfect grammar will at various points fail to express such distinctions, and this will on occasions lead to incomprehension or misunderstanding. It may often happen that the student succeeds in getting his message across (in a grammatically imperfect way) to a peer who may share his grammatical imperfections. For this reason teacher correction is also important. In the ultimate analysis he is also "correcting for content" because grammar expresses content. He is doing so with a higher level of stringency than the student's peers are perhaps able to apply; also, he is thinking beyond communicative efficacy in relation to a specific task—to future situations in which grammatical imperfections might lead to a breakdown in communication.

Conclusion

The Greek Machine exercise is, as noted earlier, suitable only for advanced students. Example 4 illustrates how the same sequence can be used at a lower level. The following is a final example of the sequence involving the production of individual sentences to describe geographical location. It is a writing exercise but could easily be modified to practise speaking.

Example 5[5]

Student A

Here are the names of four places in Britain. Their location is marked on the map.
1. Trowbridge
2. Newport
3. Harrogate
4. Fakenham

i) Use the Table overleaf to write sentences describing these places. Number the sentences as above.

ii) Show your sentences to your partner. He must write the numbers on his map.

iii) Look at your partner's map. Has he written the numbers in the right place?

Trowbridge Newport Harrogate Fakenham Mamble Oxford Wilmslow Cromer	is in	the north, the west, the south, the midlands, the east, Wales,	just	north of . . . south of . . . east of . . . south-west of . . . south-east of . . . north-west of . . .

1   Trowbridge
2   Newport
3   Harrogate
4   Fakenham

Student B

Here are the names of four places in Britain. Their location is marked on the map.

5. Mamble
6. Oxford
7. Wilmslow
8. Cromer

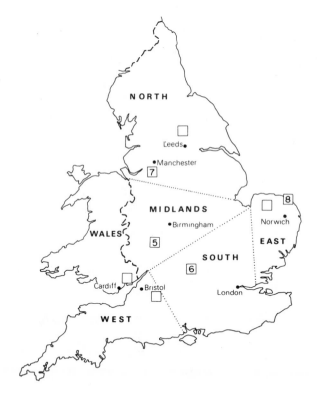

i) Use the table below to write sentences describing these places. Number the sentences as above.

Trowbridge Newport Harrogate Fakenham Mamble Oxford Wilmslow Cromer	is in	the north, the west, the south, the midlands, the east, Wales,	just	north of . . . south of . . . east of . . . south-west of . . . south-east of . . . north-west of . . .

ii) Show your sentences to your partner. He must write the numbers on his map.

iii) Look at your partner's map. Has he written the numbers in the right place?

Notes

1. From Johnson (1981).
2. Part of an exercise from Morrow and Johnson (1979).
3. In Papers 13 and 14.
4. To my knowledge, the term "jig-saw" was first used in language teaching by Marion Geddes and Gill Sturtridge. It is used in Geddes and Sturtridge (1979) for listening; White (1981) also discusses its use for reading. In both these cases the pieces of information the various students receive are closely connected, so the final result is truly a completed "jig-saw". In this paper the use of the term is slightly extended; the various pieces of information may not be closely connected; but the principle whereby students begin with different pieces of information and finish with the same information is maintained.
5. This is an adaptation of an exercise in Johnson and Morrow (1979).

Paper 16:

Teaching Appropriateness and Coherence in Academic Writing

So far in this section methodological principles have been discussed without relation to any particular teaching strategy or syllabus type, and certainly many of the techniques illustrated could be used in relation to any syllabus. The remaining papers give more attention to methodology in relation to specific types of framework. Thus this paper (and the next) concentrates on methodological issues associated with the functional syllabus. Paper 16 proposes a number of stages for the teaching of a chosen function—that of classifying. *As discussed in Section 3, there are severe theoretical problems with the functional syllabus, and a later paper (19) looks at what these problems imply in terms of methodology. The techniques presented here for functional teaching need to be assessed in terms of the alternative proposals given in Paper 19.*

This paper is a revised version of one appearing in Holden (1977).

Introduction

MOST traditional writing courses are mainly concerned with teaching grammatical accuracy. Indeed, in many cases they are simply grammar courses in (and for) the medium of writing. At the beginner and intermediate stages the emphasis is on sentence-level grammar; then as the course progresses the student learns the cohesive devices for linking sentences together to form grammatically acceptable texts.

There are of course other areas of writing skill which need to be taught. The student must also learn how to make his grammatical sentences perform functions appropriately. In ESP and academic writing contexts these functions might include *defining, classifying, comparing, contrasting, describing,* as well as many others. The student needs to be taught the linguistic means for expounding such functions. Then, at the paragraph level, he needs more than the ability to write grammatically cohesive texts. He must also learn how to write coherently, producing passages in which the sentences are linked on the level of *sense* as well as grammar. This is not only a linguistic skill (though it has a linguistic dimension, and incoherence can be the result of differences between the mother tongue and the foreign language). It also involves an organisational ability—and one which, incidentally, many native speakers do not possess.[1]

Though a complete writing programme would certainly wish to cover all writing skills, there will often be circumstances in which the course designer is forced through lack of time to give priority to some skills over others. In some situations (such as short-term pre-sessional writing programmes) this priority might be given to appropriateness and coherence.[2] There is some evidence to suggest that many university supervisors (of non-language subjects) regard incoherence as far more serious than grammatical error.[3] The subject supervisor with many overseas students may have developed such a tolerance to common grammatical mistakes (like omission of the final "s" on the third person singular simple present tense) that he virtually ceases to notice them. But he may not be prepared to accept that an instance of incoherence might have a linguistic cause, and is likely to condemn the incoherent student as stupid or disorganised.

How can functional appropriateness and coherence be taught? This short paper will consider one possible teaching sequence in relation to the function of *classifying*.[4]

Stage 1

We can begin by teaching the students some of the sentence types associated with *classifying*. Here are three.

    1. Xs may be classified according to _____

2. There are _____ types of X _____
3. Those Xs which are known as _____

Here is a short passage illustrating these sentence types being used in a classification.

Passage A
Trees may be classified according to whether they lose their leaves in winter. There are two types of tree: deciduous and evergreen. Those trees which lose their leaves in winter are known as deciduous; those which do not are known as evergreen.

It is quite easy to provide the student with information which he can use to practise writing sentences like these. We might for example give him simplified dictionary definitions:

vertebrates   —animals which have backbones
invertebrates—animals which do not have backbones
butterflies   —lepidoptera which fly by day
moths   —lepidoptera which fly by night

Here are the sentences which these four simplified definitions generate

Sentence type 1: Animals may be classified according to whether they have backbones.
Lepidoptera may be classified according to whether they fly by day.

Sentence type 2: There are two types of animal: vertebrates and invertebrates.
There are two types of lepidoptera: butterflies and moths.

Sentence type 3: Those animals which have backbones are known as vertebrates; those which do not are known as invertebrates.
Those lepidoptera which fly by day are known as butterflies; those which fly by night are known as moths.

Stage 2

What Stage 1 has done is simply teach the students some of the linguistic means English uses to classify. But the exercise is little more than a drill, and there is hardly a thought element involved. We have not shown the student how to *construct* a classification, how to make a classification *coherent*. And if he is to be able to construct his own coherent classifications, he must be able to analyse how classifications made by others have been constructed. If we analyse the rather straightforward classification found in Passage A, we find that the first sentence states what is to be classified (trees) and the criterion according to which classification is to be made (whether or not they lose their leaves in winter). The second sentence states how many classifications there are (two) and what they are called (deciduous and evergreen). In the third sentence something is said about each classification in terms of the stated criterion (deciduous lose leaves; evergreens do not). The following table summarises the passage content:

To classify	Criterion	Groups	Characterisation
Trees	Whether or not they lose their leaves in winter	1. Deciduous	Lose their leaves in winter
		2. Evergreen	Do not lose their leaves in winter

We might now ask the student to analyse other classifications in the same way. We can give him a table, exactly the same as the one above; but this time it is he who must complete it. Here are two possible passages for analysis:

Passage B
Analogue computers operate with continually varying amplitudes. The other type of computers—the digital type—do not operate on this system. They operate according to a code which cannot be varied continuously.

Passage C

The meteorologist recognises two major cloud types. They are distinguished by their composition. Thus the ice cloud is composed of ice crystals while the water cloud consists of water droplets.

Notice three important features of this exercise. One is that the *linguistic means* by which the classifications are made in Passages B and C are different from those we have drilled. For example, while we drilled "... may be classified according to ..." as the structure for giving the criterion for classification, Passage C carried the same information using "... are distinguished by ...". There are various other differences, and this is deliberate. In our lesson we will only have time to drill a few forms. But there are myriad ways of classifying in English and if we cannot drill them all, we should at least ensure that the student is exposed to as many as possible receptively.[5]

The second feature is that although each passage conveys more or less the same type of information, it does so in different sequences. The passages are *structured* differently. In Passage A the sequence is:

Sentence 1: Stating what is to be classified, and the criterion for classification.

Sentence 2: Stating how many classifications there are, and what their names are.

Sentence 3: Stating something about each classification in terms of the criterion.

In Passage C it is:

Sentence 1: Stating what is to be classified, and how many classifications there are.

Sentence 2: Stating the criterion for classification.

Sentence 3: Stating something about each classification in terms of the criterion.

Again, although we may only have time to drill one sequence, we want the student to meet as many different organisations as possible. And the more we can get him to notice and discuss these differences in organisation, the more we are helping him to understand how classifications are structured.

The third feature is related to the first two. It is that although the passages do carry more or less the same information content, sometimes that information is explicitly stated and sometimes it is implied. Passage A, for example, explicitly states, in the first sentence, what the criterion for classification is. In Passage B the criterion is implied rather than stated. This is important: students have to learn how to imply, and one way of helping them to do this is to get them to recognise implications in the writing of others.

To summarise: this stage is trying to do two things. We are teaching the student to *think* about the way classifications are structured, an essential step in the process of teaching them to write *coherent* classifications themselves. At the same time we are exposing them to a series of short texts illustrating *various* linguistic means of classifying, in *various* sequences.

Stage 3

We can now utilise the table which the students have filled in, to get them to write passages of their own. The instruction we give might be: "use the table you have just filled in to write passages about 'computers' and 'clouds'. Make the passages as much like the 'tree passage' as possible". We choose the tree passage as a model because this contains the sentence types we have drilled. Here is the computer passage rewritten in this way:

> Computers may be classified according to whether or not they operate with continually varying amplitudes. There are two types of computer: analogue and digital. Those computers which operate with continually varying amplitudes are known as analogue computers; those which do not are known as digital computers.

If time permits, we need not stop there. We could in fact get them to rewrite every passage to look like every other passage—Passage A to look like Passage B, Passage B to look like Passage C and so on. Then, as a final stage, we might simply give them some more information in table form and to get them to construct their own classification using any of the sentence patterns they have met in the lesson.

Reconstituting passages is an extremely productive technique which can be used in a number of ways. We can ask the students to rewrite a passage changing its topic, its function (what Widdowson (1973) calls "rhetorical transformation"), its style; or simply ordering the information it gives in a different way.[6]

Notes

1. Bruner (1975) speaks of an "analytic competence", which not everyone possesses, and which "involves the prolonged operation of thought processes".
2. A pre-sessional course is one for overseas students about to embark on a programme of academic study (in any subject) through the medium of a foreign language. For discussion of pre-sessional courses and materials produced for them, see Papers 4, 5 and 6.
3. This conclusion was reached at the Centre for Applied Language Studies, University of Reading, following a survey in which subject supervisors were questioned concerning overseas students' problems.
4. The sequence was much followed in the draft version of Johnson (1981). Subsequent misgivings about the earlier parts of this sequence are suggested in Paper 19.
5. A technique to increase receptive exposure in the teaching of speaking is discussed in Paper 17.
6. Exercise types of these sorts are discussed in greater detail in Paper 19.

Teaching Functional Materials: Two Practical Problems and Possible Solutions

(With Jon Roberts)

Paper 17 is in fact two papers, the second being a response to the first. In the first, Jon Roberts discusses two practical problems associated with functional teaching. Both these problems are the result of the fact, discussed at various points earlier (in Papers 7 and 11, for example), that a functional syllabus leads to the introduction of structurally different items in the same teaching unit. The second paper attempts to find solutions to these problems. It does so within the framework of the functional syllabus, and hence is in contrast to Paper 11 where the argument is that such problems should lead us to seek alternatives to the functional syllabus.

These papers appeared in Modern English Teacher, **8**, 2, 1980.

Two Practical Problems   Jon Roberts

When teaching functional coursebooks I have come across two methodological problems which are directly caused by the way the materials have been organised. These problems have arisen particularly with the functional coursebooks in which forms grouped in a unit have not been selected or graded according to principles of complexity or "learnability", as in structural courses. Instead, ungraded groups of exponents are presented together for the learner's attention.

CSDM - M

The first problem is caused by the formal diversity of exponents of a function that confront the learner. For example, in a unit on apology, the learner may see this:

I really am sorry that I am terribly sorry that	George has behaved so badly
I really must apologise about	George's behaviour

Looking at the left hand column, the learner seeks a pattern in the three forms, and thereby generalises about the grammatical system. He will then want to know whether his inferences are in fact correct. So we have this scene:

Student: John, can I say "I am really sorry."?
Teacher: Yes, sure.
Student: And "I must really apologise."?
Teacher: No, you see . . . er, oh . . . yes, it's all right
(thinks: "May I be forgiven.")
Student: And "I terribly am sorry."?
Teacher: No.
Student: Why not?

The teacher then has to present and practise not one system, as in a structurally organised coursebook, but more than one and, worse, has to contrast them to clarify restrictions on usage.

We must realise that, in trying to incorporate the three forms in one system or find out reasons for formal diversity, the learner is not being perverse, nor is he merely conditioned by prior experience of structural coursebooks. On the contrary, he is using an essential learning strategy that enables us to handle information. As Bruner (1972) characterises it, two of these strategies are:

1. We are connective. Invariant (i.e. stable or unchanging) features are put together as working models . . . .
2. We are alarmed by deviance. We have special alarm mechanisms for events that deviate beyond a certain amount from our models.

Applying these strategies to language learning, the learner will need to perceive a pattern in the "data" presented and will try to form rules on the data given. Inconsistencies in the restrictions that apply to forms presented together will "set off the alarm". The learners are likely to demand clarification of each system from which these different forms derive so that the new information can be integrated with their own interim rule systems. The net effect of grouping forms that derive from different systems may be to commit the teacher to lengthy contrastive grammatical exposition, quite the opposite of the original goal.

The second problem relates to stylistic variation and appropriacy. We know that one function can be expounded in a wide variety of forms. Expressing approval, for example, could range from "Great." to "I really think that that was a superb . . . if I may say so." In one advanced level functional coursebook (Jones, 1977), for example, eleven ways of asking permission, graded in order of politeness, are presented together:

> I'm going to leave early/I thought I might leave early/I'd like to leave early/Alright if I leave early?/Anyone mind if I leave early?/D'you mind if I leave early?/Is it alright if I leave early?/Would it be alright if I left early?/Would you mind if I left early?/I wonder if I could possibly leave early?/I hope you don't mind, but would it be at all possible for me to leave early?

Whether the coursebook presents eleven exponents or only two, the problem is still there:

> Student: John, when should I say "Do you mind if . . .?", and when "Alright if I . . .?"

No two exponents are exactly the same in terms of when it is appropriate to use them. If they were, we would not need both exponents. The discrimination between rival possibilities may be quite gross, as above, or so fine grained as to be beyond all but native speaker intuition. However, the difference has to be recognised in the materials and in the classroom.

That is the problem, and a function coursebook cannot evade it because of the status of context in indicating language function. We can only recognise how a form is functioning if we have access to the facts of the context of utterance, and so the functional coursebook must present all these relevant facts. However, the writer cannot then allow learners to think that the different forms (the two or the eleven) are interchangeable and that selection is in no way affected by context. That would falsify the facts.

Not all students will ask directly for stylistic information as in my example, but the teacher will still have to cope with the problem for example when using role play and having to decide whether to ignore or correct inappropriate choices. Neither writer nor teacher will be able to evade the context–exponent selection problem, and look again at the list of eleven exponents above to see how severe the problem is. First, it is very hard, perhaps impossible, to grade such a large set of exponents according to a single criterion. The eleven are not homogeneous ("Anyone mind ...?" is situationally different from "Is it alright ...?") and not all native speakers would agree on degrees of politeness. (Is "Alright if...?" more polite than "I'd like to....?"). Second, if we accept that the eleven are all different in terms of appropriateness, then it suggests that the teacher is committed to their separate contextualisation and practice. Not only does this lead to a great deal of *description* of contexts, *discussion* of selection and relatively little actual *practice*, but also it requires a bilingual's proficiency from the non-native speaker teacher. Third, one can doubt whether it is reasonable to ask the learner not only to recognise stylistic differences but also to produce contextually appropriate utterances to a level of discrimination implied by the presentation of many forms. All these problems will tend to produce a great deal of *speaking about* functions and less actual use.

In summary, the functional course must in its nature present sets of formally and stylistically diverse exponents. For reasons given above, this tends to force the teacher into adopting the role of explainer/source of knowledge, to the exclusion of his prime intention: to enable meaningful practice focused on the meaning and the effect of utterances.

Possible Solutions[1]   Keith Johnson

I SHOULD like to look at these two problems mainly from the standpoint of the materials producer. Examples like the one Jon Roberts gives from a unit on apology certainly do occur in functional materials. Why? One reason may be that the materials writer has simply misjudged the grammatical competence of his students. A main aim of many functional materials is to "activate" previously learned grammar and for this reason many of them are of the "one-off intermediate or above" variety. In this situation it is often very difficult for the writer to be sure exactly what structures the students have already mastered. He may make mistakes.

So it may be that in the case of Jon Roberts' example the writer (mistakenly) assumes that the students have mastered the "really/terribly" distinction, and wishes to focus attention on the difference between *"that" + sentence* and *"about" + NP*. If so, he is (or thinks he is) following the sound pedagogic principle of 'introducing no more than one new thing at a time'.

But what does the teacher do when he finds a functional book assumes grammatical competence which the students do not in fact have? One solution is, of course, to switch to a simpler book. Alternatively, if the students only occasionally meet unknown structures, the teacher can cover them as they occur; or he can simply omit the offending structures. So in the case of the apology example, we might either launch into a session explaining and practising the "really/terribly" distinction, or practise apologising without these words.

But this is only part of an answer, and there may be a second reason why the apology example occurs. It may reflect the material writer's decision not to follow a structural grading (or to follow the pedagogic principle mentioned above). He might justify this standpoint in theoretical terms, referring perhaps to the way a child learns its first language. What Jon Roberts calls "formal diversity" is just what the child meets in everyday life—and still manages to apply Bruner's strategies successfully.[2]

Whatever our views on the parallel between first and foreign language learning, many of us would wish to express grave dissatisfaction with the kind of rigid structural control which characterised much past language teaching. We welcome the relaxation of this rigid control, and in doing so we are surely conceding that the learner may be exposed to "variance" and "deviance" without too much damage being done. It could be said that we have come to place greater faith in the ability of the strategies characterised by Bruner to operate with data which (like the data which a child learning its first language receives) is "variant" and "deviant".

A belief of this kind does of course leave itself open to the sort of criticism Jon Roberts discusses. Any argument for less control over language presented immediately invokes cries of, "but what if the student doesn't know X, Y or Z?" And I think most of us overcome this problem by selectively focusing our students' attention. We emphasise some points and are prepared (like teachers in all subjects) to skate over others which occur in the lesson but which we do not at that moment wish to concentrate on.

Two standpoints have been discussed above, and they are in conflict. According to the first, no more than one new thing should be introduced at a time; and according to the second we should relax control over what we introduce. Teachers may (quite justifiably) see wisdom in both points of view. How, then, can they be reconciled? There is perhaps room for both, but at different points in the teaching operation. Jon Roberts' apology example has all the appearance of a presentation stage for language to be intensively practised—and that is perhaps what is most worrying about it. At this stage and for language to be given this treatment there is surely a strong argument in favour of control over the amount of new language to be introduced. But at other stages of the lesson where language is given for less intensive practice, then we can perhaps tolerate more "formal diversity".

So I would suggest that the issue depends on what we intend to do with the introduced language. When we intend to concentrate intensively on our language point, then there is much to be said for its clear presentation "uncluttered" by too many new pieces of language which will merely complicate the issue. But there is still a place in the classroom for "formal diversity". It would be to misrepresent things, surely, if the existence of the two strategies Bruner characterises were used to justify the kind of rigid control over exposure to language which took place in the past.

Jon Roberts' two problems have a common base. They both involve the question: "How many language points can be made per lesson, and how thoroughly?" One has again to admit that Jon Roberts' second problem does exist, and has indeed led to the criticism that some functional materials are little more than elaborate phrasebooks.[3] It is certainly healthy to be reminded that functional materials can indeed end up talking too much *about* the language. Because functional materials deal with *language use*, this does not necessarily imply that they always teach *use of language*. We may make a perfectly respectable functional syllabus the basis for a series of sociolinguistic lectures on strategies for *greeting*, *inviting*, etc., in English. At the end of the lecture course we can claim to have dealt with language use, but the student may still not be able to *greet*, *invite*, etc., in communicative situations. The moral is that "being functional" is not enough; our degree of success will depend as much on the sophistication of our methodology as on the pedigree of our syllabus.

The utility of the kind of "listing approach" Jon Roberts exemplifies depends surely on what we wish it to achieve. It seems incontrovertible that when covering any language function we are committed to presenting and intensively practising some chosen exponents. This also involves a commitment to contextualise them separately and to point out the kinds of situations, role relationships, degrees of formality, etc., they are appropriate to. It would be folly to practise "Hi." intensively without making it somehow clear this is not how one greets the Queen.

For this purpose the "listing approach" seems unsuited. But the "commitment to differentiate" does pose a problem, because it is so time consuming. If we are not careful, we find that in our "Asking Permission" unit we have differentiated and practised two or three forms only. Can we then really say we have taught *asking permission?* Surely we have a further commitment, to provide some kind of breadth of coverage of the function in question.

This leads one to think that there is a place somewhere in the lesson for something like the "listing approach". Here we would introduce exponents, perhaps only for receptive learning and with little concern for contextual differentiation. The exercise below (from Morrow and Johnson, 1979) shows one way of handling this.

   i) Who says these things? In what situations?

a. It would help if you could hold the torch for me a second and I'll see if I can find it.	Hold _____	?
b. I wonder if you could move your head a little. I can't see.	Could you _____	?
c. I want you to run round and tell John to come back home immediately.	Run _____	?

d. As it's raining, I thought you might   You couldn't __ ?
   collect him by car.

e. What *is* the time? Mine's stopped.   Could you _____ ?

f. I like it better over there. Do me a   Move_____ ?
   favour and move it for me, dear.

g. I wonder if you could change it. I   You couldn't __ ?
   like to have a clean tablecloth.

h. Let me borrow yours, George. I've   Could I _____ ?
   only got a pencil.

ii) Make new sentences using the words on the right.

The exponents on the left are new to the student, and part (i) of the exercise asks him to think about contextual differentiation (in fairly crude terms). Then in part (ii) he revamps the sentences using exponents already practised and differentiated. The result of following this strategy over the lesson as a whole is that the student will be able to use a small number of exponents in contextually appropriate ways, but has also been exposed to many more. I would argue strongly that to do one of these things to the total exclusion of the other is a mistake.

The exercise above involves introducing additional exponents for receptive learning. But to end on what is perhaps a controversial note: maybe what we need is a concept of "grades of productive learning". We should, in other words, perhaps recognise categories of "half learned language"—language which has been introduced and practised productively, but not to the extent that we can say it is fully mastered. This would certainly replicate what occurs when we learn a language in a "natural" environment, where at any given time we will find ourselves using language not fully acquired. We are often fond of saying that whereas in the past all language was taught in relation to all the four skills, today we distinguish between receptive and productive learning. Perhaps we should now go one step further and accept that not all language taught productively need, on introduction, be taught to the same degree of proficiency. We may wish to "half teach" an item in Unit 7, and finish off the job in Unit 14![4]

Notes

1. Problems similar to the ones Jon Roberts considered are discussed in theoretical terms in Paper 11. See Paper 19 also for discussion of the need to contextualise.
2. See Paper 10 for discussion of this standpoint.
3. As argued in Paper 11.
4. This relates to the concept of "incubation" discussed in Paper 12.

Paper 18:

The "Deep End" Strategy in Communicative Language Teaching

One way in which teachers have responded to the need for a "task-orientated" language teaching has been to adopt a strategy in which the student is first placed in a situation where he needs to use language, and is then taught the language he requires. One version of this strategy is Paper 12's procedural syllabus; another is the "deep end" strategy described here. A theme recurring in this volume is the need to develop a coherent specification of what is involved in communication performance, and to devise approaches based on this. A particularly appealing feature of the deep end strategy is that it recognises the importance of "risk taking" in learning how to communicate, and provides a framework for its development.

This paper was published in MEXTESOL Journal **4**, *2, 1980.*

In a recent paper,[1] Brumfit suggests that a lasting impact of communicative language teaching may involve a change in traditional classroom procedure, as below:

	Stage 1	Present
Traditional procedure	Stage 2	Drill
	Stage 3	Practise in context

Communicative procedure	Stage 1	Students communicate with available resources
	Stage 2	Teacher presents items shown to be necessary
	Stage 3	Drill if necessary

The example on the following pages[2] illustrates one way in which this second procedure might manifest itself in materials (though it will be argued later that this example in fact compromises with the procedure as represented above). The aim of this paper is to consider advantages and disadvantages of the communicative procedure, which for obvious reasons will be referred to as the "deep end strategy".

The strategy departs from tradition (and will offend traditionalists) in a number of ways. It reverses, for example, the usual sequence of "reception to production" in which the student's initial role is that of listener or reader (Stage 1) and only later (Stages 2 and 3) that of producer. In the deep end strategy the student first produces; he listens or reads only at Stage 2. The strategy also reverses the sequence of "atomistic to holistic language practice" since in it the student first practises the entire behaviour and only later (Stage 3) drills items in isolation.[3]

But perhaps the most important departure from tradition is that at Stage 1 of the strategy the student is placed in a situation where he may need to use language not yet taught. Indeed, it is a central characteristic of the strategy that the student is taught at Stages 2 and 3 language which he needed at Stage 1. "Teaching", that is, succeeds rather than precedes "use". An important implication is that, because at Stage 1 the student will almost certainly find his available resources inadequate, he is likely to make mistakes.

In this last mentioned respect the strategy contrasts sharply with established behaviourist procedures of "shaping" which seek to avoid situations in which student error might occur. But it is precisely for this reason that the strategy provides opportunity to practise skills important to the acquisition of communicative competence (and which the behaviourist procedures ignore). These skills involve the ability to search for circumlocutions when the appropriate language item is not

5 Inviting

SECTION A: ORAL PRACTICE

1 What would you say?

Peter and Barbara have been out together. Peter wants to take her out again tomorrow.

They arrive at Barbara's house. They've both had a good time. What do they say?

Peter invites her. She accepts.

They make arrangements before saying goodnight.

2

Practise inviting in these situations:

i)   You haven't seen your boyfriend/girlfriend for at least a day! Maybe he/she can have lunch with you tomorrow.

ii) Your landlady took you out last week. Maybe you should ask her out once. There's an Agatha Christie play on at the theatre on Friday.

iii) Jon's having a party this Saturday. A new French girl has just arrived in your class. Maybe she will come with you.

iv) You want to go to the cinema on Monday evening, but you have no one to go with. Ask a classmate.

v)   You and your friends are leaving England next week, and you are all having a dinner party together. You want to invite your teacher.

3   a) Here is your diary for next week. Decide what you are doing on three days. Write it in your diary.

Sunday	
Monday	
Tuesday	
Wednesday	
Thursday	
Friday	
Saturday	

known; to perceive when the listener has not understood what was said and to struggle to rephrase it; to search the memory for items learned long ago—or half-learned, or just met in passing. The ability to muster in this way imperfect linguistic resources to a communicative end is a fundamental one. It is one which until he reaches high proficiency, the student will have to employ constantly and quickly—constantly because so often as he attempts to express himself in the foreign language he will find his resources inadequate; quickly because the constraints which hold in a conversational situation demand rapid response. The deep end strategy should help to develop in the student a type of confidence essential to learning a foreign language: the confidence to attempt to say something which he knows that he does not really know how to say.

The strategy's implicit recognition of such skills is what makes it "communicative". It fits well within a language teaching aiming to develop fluency (as the ability to perform skills like these quickly) as well as accuracy, and it can only do so because the "free communication" occurs at Stage 1. If Stage 3 of the traditional procedure does involve an element of risk taking this is often by accident rather than design. The teacher assumption is that the language used at Stage 3 will be the language learned at Stages 1 and 2. The procedure has been set up precisely with this link in mind. The student will, moreover, probably share this assumption and can therefore be forgiven for viewing Stage 3 as a vehicle for practising Stage 1 and 2 language rather than as an exercise in true communication. He will, in Widdowson's (1978a) terms, see it as practice in "usage" rather than "use". This may well in turn result in stultified interaction as the students struggle to fit what they want to say into the language they have just learned. Free practice in the "deep end" strategy is likely to be more "natural", if less accurate, than in the traditional strategy.

A further advantage of the communicative procedure is its diagnostic value, for both teacher and student. It tells the teacher what the student does and does not know, and this provides the framework for subsequent teaching. Information on what the student knows ensures that time will not be wasted on items already mastered, while information on areas of weakness provide a means for making Stage 2 and 3 teaching needs-specific. From the student's point of view, Stage 1 draws attention to areas where available resources are inadequate, and this should have considerable motivational value. Thus Stages 2 and 3 will not only be, but will be seen to be, needs-specific.

Another attractive feature of the strategy as exemplified in the exercises given earlier is that it is flexible as regards student level. Since any function may be expounded in various more or less complex ways, students at a variety of levels may do Exercise 1 above. Thus with low level students Picture 2 may elicit:

Peter: Can you come to the pictures tomorrow?

Barbara: Yes.

while a more advanced group may produce:

Peter: Listen, Barbara. There's a new play on at the New Theatre next week.

Barbara: Oh? What is it?

Peter: It's Tom Stoppard's "Dirty Linen". You haven't seen it, have you?

Barbara: No.

Peter: I've heard it's very good.

Barbara: Well, it sounds interesting.

Peter: Yes. Anyway, how would you like to go and see it? I planned to go myself anyway.

Barbara: Well, yes. I'd like that. But I've got quite a lot on next week. When . . .?

Exercise 2 has a similar flexibility; low level students may concentrate on one of the given exponents ("Shall we . . .?", perhaps) while higher levels can practise them all.

If we now forget the exercises given earlier and concentrate on the strategy as represented in the diagram at the beginning of this paper, we find that it has one serious disadvantage which poses the teacher and/or materials producer with a considerable problem. For if students are given a genuine opportunity to communicate freely at Stage 1, it follows that we shall be unable to predict what will be said and what shortcomings will be revealed. Hence it will be impossible to prepare in advance the content of Stage 2 and 3 teaching. There are teaching situations in which this may not matter. In them the students would communicate with available resources and the teacher would identify areas of need. He would then go to a resources room which would contain banks of drills to cover all possible areas of need. He would return to the classroom with appropriate materials and proceed with the lesson. It is a scenario requiring both huge resources and nerves of steel—huge resources because the banks of drills would indeed have to be exhaustive, and nerves of steel because the teacher would have to be willing to give lessons with very little advanced preparation.[4]

In many teaching situations where huge resources and nerves of steel are lacking this procedure would be impossible, though this is not to say that it is an undesirable objective to work towards. Note that the procedure does indeed involve a drastic change in the role of materials. They cease to provide a set of exercises to work through in prescribed sequence, and become a bank of resources to select from.

If the deep end strategy is to be used in general teaching situations, some means of predicting and circumscribing Stage 2 and 3 activities needs to be found. One possible solution is illustrated in the exercises given earlier. In these the materials producer presents at Stage 2 language which he predicts the student "may have wanted to use" at Stage 1. This is a compromise because the lesson proceeds on the basis of predicted rather than necessarily shown needs, and the solution thus loses diagnostic value. It may happen, in Exercise 1 given earlier, that the student uses none of the forms presented in Exercise 2 but invites with the exponent "let's" which he gets wrong. This invalidates the utility of Exercise 2 as it stands. It may also happen, more seriously, that the student *invites* correctly, but *makes arrangements* incorrectly, again invalidating the utility of Exercise 2. But note that in the first of these eventualities, adaptation is possible. Because the cues in Exercise 2 are situational, they can be used to practise any exponent of invitation including ones not presented in the box. The solution is a compromise, but it is one which does at least allow materials to be produced and hence some predictability to be given to the lesson.

A second solution, useful for the teaching of writing to unilingual groups, is the following:[5]

Stage 1

Students are given an
(imperfect) essay written
by a member of the same
language group

Stage 2

Students rewrite the essay
correcting the mistakes

Stage 3

Students compare their
version with a model
version

Stage 4

Students work at their own
speed through a given
"bank of drills", selecting
those calculated to
eliminate the mistakes they
failed to recognise at
Stage 2

Stage 5

Students write an essay on
a connected topic

This solution retains diagnostic value since at Stage 4 the student is only drilling items he has failed to correct at Stage 2. And because the students' production at Stage 2 is based on an initial imperfect essay, the materials producer has a finite number of errors to deal with, and hence drills to provide. These drills constitute a bank and no one student would probably need to do them all. But the solution compromises on another aspect of the strategy—the "initial communication with available resources" is based on a piece of writing presented to the student; it is thus neither entirely free nor (since it is an exercise essentially in error correction) does it practise all the processes involved in composition.

To return finally to the question of level. To many teachers the deep end strategy will share with other communicative approaches a lack of guided control over student exposure to, and practice of, language. This will suggest to them that it is only really suitable at the post-intermediate level. Certainly the strategy invites the specific question: to what extent will communication at Stage 1 be possible when the student (at beginner or near beginner level) has no available resources? Experimentation, along the lines of Savignon (1972) may reveal that the strategy is possible even with beginners, but this (empirical) question must remain unanswered until the experimentation is done. More certainly, the approach will have advantages for the student who has learned grammar in a traditional way, and needs it to be "activated".[6] Given that much of past language teaching has tended to be slowly incremental and to delay activation of structural knowledge, it may well be that an approach which follows a short, intensive "crash" structural course with immediate activation by the deep end strategy will be successful. In this approach the student would be introduced to structures in a traditional way; but the time spent on non-communicative practice would be minimised and the structures would be "recycled" as soon as possible within the communicative framework of the deep end strategy.

Notes

1. Brumfit (1978). These procedures are also discussed in Brumfit (1979).
2. From Johnson and Morrow (1979).
3. Because it reverses the "atomistic to holistic" sequence it relates to the methodological solutions discussed in Paper 10.
4. One way in which the teacher may extend preparation time is by doing Stage 1 on one day and the subsequent stages on the next.
5. The present writer has been developing materials along these lines for use by Spanish and Portuguese speakers.
6. Johnson and Morrow (1979) is subtitled "a language activation course". The theme of whether a one- or two-stage operation is appropriate has recurred at several points in the book. See particularly the final paragraphs of Paper 1, Papers 9 and 11.

Paper 19:

Communicative Writing Practice and Aristotelian Rhetoric

This paper is of central importance to the collection. In some respects it goes together with the Section 3 papers, and certainly needs to be read with these (particularly Paper 11) in mind. But because it brings together a number of points made throughout the collection—concerning methodology as well as syllabus design—it has been placed at the end. The paper is academic in tone. Although it has theoretical sections, the approach it is advocating was the result of a materials production experience and was hence developed with practical concerns very much in mind.

This paper was delivered at the 12th Annual Conference of the Canadian Council of Teachers of English, held in Ottawa (May, 1979), on the topic of "Learning to Write". It is scheduled to be published in a collection of selected papers from the conference (Longman).

1. Introduction

THIS paper[1] is concerned with an important aspect of the communicative skill. It will argue that communicative events, as responses to relatively "unique" combinations of stimuli, are in themselves non-stereotyped (though of course derived from sets of rules which are discoverable). It will claim that notional/functional approaches which identify discrete semantic areas and simply present a set of exponents for each, are therefore severely inadequate as overall teaching strategies. It will attempt to outline an approach which takes into account the non-stereotyped nature of communicative events.[2]

The specific "universe of discourse" for this paper is the teaching of academic writing, and what is said stems from experience in producing and piloting a set of academic writing materials.[3] Throughout, the term "semantic syllabus" is used as an umbrella term for any syllabus specified in notional and/or functional categories; the word "utterance" is used for any stretch of discourse, in written or spoken medium; "context" is used to describe the complex set of linguistic and non-linguistic features within which an utterance takes place.

2. Communicative Events

An area of study possessing a rich literature as yet comparatively untapped by the applied linguist is that of skills psychology. Welford (1958) describes the skilled performer (or "receptor") as:

> ...a kind of calculating machine capable of receiving several different inputs and producing an output which is derived from the various input parameters acting in concert. Such a system results in a response which is unique on each occasion, although it is determinate and based on constraints which are, at least in principle, discoverable.

Applied to a skill like playing tennis, the various input parameters leading to the response of playing a single stroke would include speed of the ball, position of the receiving player, position of his opponent, etc. Since the response would be to a unique combination of input parameters, it would itself be a "unique" event.

Applied to a skill like language the input might be characterised in terms of the various parameters to which the utterance (as output) must conform. In Hymes's (1970) programmatic and thus inevitably general terms these parameters are four: the appropriate, the possible, the feasible, the performed. Subdividing his "appropriate" into "appropriateness to intent" and "appropriateness to context" we arrive at the diagram overleaf to exemplify the aspect of skilled behaviour Welford speaks of:[4] In this diagram, the number of boxes appearing under "intents" and "context" is arbitrary, but more than one in each case, to express the fact that an utterance will have more than one intent, and must conform to very many more than one parameter of context.

The diagram indicates a number of things. The one to be considered

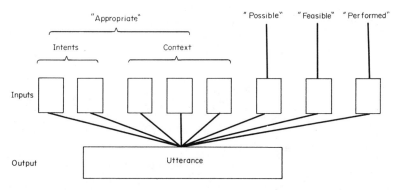

here is that a large part of any communicative language teaching must be concerned with the expression of intents within contexts. In terms of the teaching of writing this seems to lead towards an Aristotelian view of rhetoric, defined by Grierson (1945)[5] as "the study of how to express oneself correctly and effectively, bearing in mind the nature of the language we use, the subject we are speaking or writing about, the kind of audience we have in view . . . and the purpose, which last is in the main determinant". The quotation relates well to the diagram given earlier—the "nature of the language" falling within the "possible" box; the "subject" (topic) and "audience" being parameters of context; and "purpose" being "intent". Within such an Aristotelian rhetoric (and communicative language teaching) our concept of "good writing" must be one in which the student is able to (and is judged by others according to whether he does) successfully express his intents within contexts.

That a communicative language teaching has this aim is by now generally accepted, and most attempts to realise it take what might loosely be called "categories of intent" ("functions") as their starting point and teach language items in relation to each. But such an approach can only succeed if it is sensitive to the nature of the relationships which hold between intents and the utterances which convey them. Two points may be made about these relationships. The first is that context plays an important role in mediating them. It is by now generally accepted that while some utterances obligingly proclaim their communicative intent (*promising* sentences which begin "I promise . . .", *defining* sentences which include the structure ". . . may be defined as . . ", for example), most utterances are not of this type. We rely on context (and the set of presuppositions, felicity conditions, etc., it carries) for the interpretation of communicative value. Thus we will interpret utterances like "the adder is a poisonous snake" variously as classification, descriptive statement, warning, according to context. This has clear implications for the teaching of reading, but no less for writing. The way we express intents depends crucially on the contexts we are to express them in; our ability to express intents depends crucially on our ability to perceive how we will be interpreted in context.

The second point is that these sets of relationships—intent/utterance and context/utterance—are both delicate and complex. They are delicate because a slight change in intent will necessitate a change in utterance—the "marks on the page" will have to change. Similarly, a slight change in context (perhaps involving a change in the set of presuppositions) will render inappropriate an utterance previously appropriate. The relationships are complex because they are realised, not by rules involving binary correct/incorrect decisions, but by ones relating to felicity conditions, topic-comment relationships, distribution of information, and so on.

These two points are important because they indicate that communicative events are non-stereotyped not merely because of the *number* of parameters which derive them (which is, in essence, Welford's point); but also because of the complex and delicate way in which those parameters which are crucial exert their control.

3. General Implications for the Teaching of Writing

There are two general implications of this view of communication, one negative and one positive. The negative implication is that any approach (and most "notional" approaches have been of this type) which identifies specific areas of use, presents several forms associated with each, perhaps differentiating the forms crudely in terms of some scale such as formality-informality, has severe inadequacies.[6] The kind of problems such an approach meets may be exemplified within the area of *defining*. It may be that a needs analysis isolates (1) and (2), exemplified in (3) and (4) as profitable exponents to teach for this function:

1. An X $\begin{smallmatrix} \text{who} \\ \text{which} \end{smallmatrix}$ _____ is known as Y.

2. A Y is an X $\begin{smallmatrix} \text{who} \\ \text{which} \end{smallmatrix}$ _____.

3. A person who does not live in one fixed place is known as a vagrant.

4. A vagrant is a person who does not live in one fixed place.

As soon as the materials producer attempts to present and set up practice for these forms he is made aware of their non-equivalence on various levels. On one level is the fact that a cat is an animal which has four legs, but an animal which has four legs is not known as a cat. Failure to realise the non-equivalence of these exponents on this level leads students to produce both (5) and (6):

5. Zoology is a science which studies living things.

6. *A science which studies living things is known as zoology.

and one is left to explain why the indefinite article, appropriate in (3), is inappropriate in (6)—though it could be replaced by "one", as in (7):

7. One science which studies living things is known as zoology.

The two exponents are also non-equivalent as regards contextual appropriateness. Thus (because of the rules governing the distribution of "old" and "new" information in discourse, with "old" information usually opening a sentence) only one of the following contexts could take both (3) and (4):

8. The vagrant population of America is large. _____.

9. A large number of people in America do not live in one fixed place. _____.

10. _____. There are many vagrants in America.

Examples like this—and of course part of the point is the frequency with which the materials producer will meet them—indicate the healthy distrust for generalisation which the non-stereotyped nature of communicative events should breed. They argue against a strategy which provides a set of exponents and which implicitly or explicitly makes a statement like "This is how we define (classify, exemplify, etc.) in

English." They argue instead for (the second, positive, implication) an approach which begins with pieces of discourse exemplifying a specific set of writer intentions and a specific set of contextual features for the exponent to be taught; which makes statements like, "This is how the writer has defined in this set of circumstances.", and explores why he has done so in that particular way.

4. Aspects of the Second Approach

What does this second approach imply in terms of pedagogic procedures? Two related implications will be considered here. The first is that any communicative writing course would have a large "analysis component".[7] This component would present examples of discourse and would lead the student to explore the complex, delicate and crucial relationships holding between its constituent utterances, their contexts and intents. The component would be large for the reasons discussed above—because the relationships are complex and delicate and can only be elucidated by considerable exploration; because many of the language points we wish to make can only be explained by careful consideration of contextual features; because high exposure to stretches of discourse seems the only valid strategy for approaching their constituent, non-stereotyped events.

Much of this "analysis component" would consist of what is traditionally called reading comprehension, and might cover the following types of activity:

(a) Exploring Intent/Utterance Relationships[8]

E.g.—asking the student to identify the writer's main point in a paragraph (or larger/smaller unit). Since the intent of an utterance is interpreted in relation to context, we should presumably establish with our students the intent of larger units of discourse *before* looking at smaller ones (i.e. we question about passage intent before paragraph intent; paragraph intent before sentence intent, etc.).

—various other types of comprehension questions (including true/false exercises) which focus on the writer's communicative intent.

(b) Exploring Context/Utterance Relationships

E.g.—cloze procedures in which the student must supply (with or without the aid of a multiple-choice selection) missing words or sentences. That is, he is given a context and must decide what utterances are appropriate to it. One way of cueing this is to tell the student what functions the missing portions expound.

—provide the utterance and ask about its context ("What has the writer just said?" and "What is he about to say?").

Some of the techniques under (c) below are also useful for exploring context/utterance relationships.

(c) Exploring Organisation

E.g.—forward and backward speculation:

i) The student looks at the first paragraph of a passage, covering the rest with a piece of blank paper. He is asked to speculate on how the passage might continue. He then looks at the second paragraph and compares his speculation with what is actually written. He continues in this way through the passage.

ii) The same technique may be used but with the student beginning with the last paragraph of the passage. He then speculates on what comes before.

iii) Donley (1976) proposes a technique whereby the teacher dictates the first sentence of a paragraph, asks for speculation on the second sentence, dictates it and so on through the paragraph.

The present writer has found that with all these techniques it is usually necessary to provide the student with some clue as to the overall content of the passage or paragraph. This may be provided by a set of unordered sentences stating what points are made in the passage, or by an unordered list of the functions which the passage/paragraph expounds.

(a)   i) —asking a student to add given sentences (or larger/smaller units) to the passage. With a judicious choice of sentences to add, this can lead the student to lengthy consideration of how the passage is organised.

—functional ordering. The student is given a set of randomly ordered "functional labels" (e.g. comparing, defining, classifying) which describe what the writer says in the passage. The student must order these.

This can be the first stage in a parallel writing exercise which continues as follows:

ii) —The student does the same for a second passage. This passage includes the same functions as Passage 1, but expounded in a different order.

iii) —The student rewrites Passage 2 to expound the functions as they are ordered in Passage 1. That is, he rewrites Passage 2 to have the same organisation as Passage 1. Parallel writing can be used at several levels. At its most complex it can involve detailed analysis of discourse and the reorganisation of passages.

(b)   —sentence ordering. The student is given a sequence of mixed sentences to put in order. This is particularly successful if presented as a game, with each sentence written on a card. The students in groups are given sets of cards which they must order in sequence.

If the sentences are presented with cohesive devices missing, nouns replacing pronouns, etc., the exercise can be extended to become a sentence combining one.

As several of these techniques exemplify, the "analysis component" feeds naturally into, and does itself have elements of, production practice. Our initial questions may be of the sort: "What is the writer saying here?", "Why does he say it like that?", "Why doesn't he say it like this?" and "How is the passage organised?", etc. But we may then move naturally into questions involving an element of production—such as

"How would the writer have put it if he had wanted to say something slightly different?" and "How would the writer have put it in a slightly different context?" In exercises like these (which might be dubbed " 'If' exercises") we suggest a change in intent or context and ask how it would affect the utterance. " 'If' exercises" represent a highly productive technique and may result in the complete reorganisation of a passage. Examples are given later.

These observations lead to a second implication, related to the first, that a highly fruitful approach to communicative writing is "discourse based". In such an approach, the starting point for production exercises is pieces of discourse which the student is asked to do operations on. One major appeal of this approach is its specificity. We are providing a specific set of utterance-intent-context relationships embodying a specific set of presuppositions and felicity conditions, we explore these in the "analysis component"; we then require specific tasks to be done on them.

The following techniques exemplify the types of operations the student can be asked to perform on pieces of discourse (which he has previously analysed in some depth):

(a) Inserting Information

    i) The technique of giving sentences (or larger/smaller units) to be added to a passage has already been mentioned.

    ii) As a (more demanding) alternative, pieces of information in the form of a "list of points" can be given. The student must not only decide *where* to make these points, but *how* to make them also. With ingenuity it is possible to ask the student to add a number of points to a passage using a discrete number of language forms. For example, the student can be asked to add five "concession points" to a passage, using "although" (and/or other chosen exponents).

(b) Subtracting Information

As with the insertion of information, asking the student to take a piece of information out of a passage can lead to substantial reorganisation of its content.

Note the naturalness of both these types of task. They are the types of operation which every writer of academic prose is constantly undertaking.

(c) Reorganising a Passage to Make the Same Points in a Different Order

One possibility is the following sequence:
  i) Students read a passage and take notes (or complete a set of skeleton notes).
  ii) The students are then given a set of alternative notes which make the same points but in a different order. The students are asked to pinpoint the differences in the two sets of notes.
  iii) Students then rewrite the passage following the second set of notes.

Often however it is sufficient simply to provide a new introductory (or concluding) sentence as the stimulus for reorganisation.

In these forms the exercises may provide useful practice in cohesion and coherence, but they remain mechanical unless the student is given a reason for reorganisation. An Aristotelian rhetoric would presumably require, where possible, the differentiation of alternative organisations in terms of intent and effect. The techniques mentioned below are less mechanical in this respect.

(d) "Rhetorical Transformations"

This type of exercise, discussed in Widdowson (1973) involves rewriting a stretch of discourse to change its communicative value. For example, rewriting a set of instructions as a description. (e) and (f) below elaborate this technique.

(e) Changing Standpoint/Point of Emphasis

Rewriting a passage to convey the same information but to argue a different point or to change degrees of emphasis.

(f) **Changing "style"**

For example, changing a lecture transcript into a piece of academic prose. This may involve considerable replanning if (as many are) the lecture is loosely organised and repetitive.

To conclude this section by reviewing the issues from a slightly different angle: a central tenet of communicative language teaching is that it should provide practice at expression intents within contexts. One widespread (and fruitful) response to this has been a partial shift of role on the part of materials producer and teacher. They have tended to become initiators of language behaviour, following the principle that, "We set up a situation in which we provide the student with something to say; we let him say it, then we examine what he has said in relation to what he wanted to say." A pedagogic problem this approach poses is to set up initial situations in a way which is specific enough to lead to fruitful discussion and use of language by the students. A central feature of the approach expounded here is that it provides initial "situations" in the form of pieces of discourse written for specific audiences to achieve specific purposes.

5. Observations on Syllabus Design

What are the implications of such an approach for syllabus design? Three observations will be made.

i) The approach leads towards that followed in the teaching of receptive skills, where we begin with a piece of discourse (a taped dialogue or a reading passage) which we exploit in a number of probably unconnected ways. For example, we might use a dialogue to explore questions of pronunciation, vocabulary, grammar, appropriacy. We would certainly consider it cost-ineffective to exploit a long dialogue in only one way, and the approach thus involves a "cluster of activities around a stretch of discourse". A similar approach for the teaching of production skills would move away from the reasonably entrenched practice of covering one discrete (functional, structural) area per teaching unit. It moves towards an approach touching on many (probably unconnected) areas per unit.

ii) A second, connected, observation concerns the status of the syllabus. In such an approach it tends to lose its status as predeterminer of ordering. Traditionally it is at the syllabus design stage that the sequence of presentation of language items is established. In the suggested approach the selected pieces of discourse would to some extent determine unit content and hence overall sequence. The syllabus would then become largely an inventory of items to be covered on the course as a whole; it would function as a "check list" against which we "tick off" points covered, rather than as an "algorithm" which imposes a predetermined ordering.

iii) The third observation concerns syllabus content. It is today increasingly remarked that the procedure (largely followed in semantic syllabus design) whereby we select semantic categories and specify a set of surface structures associated with each, is fundamentally behaviouristic. The procedure certainly seems open to the kind of criticism that Chomsky made of Skinner—to the extent that by providing specific sets of surface structures as responses to the "situations" (as stimuli) in which the student will want to use language, it is tacitly subscribing to a simplistic S–R view of language behaviour. Indeed, the central argument of this paper is that such a procedure dangerously over-simplifies.

We seem to need for language use what Chomsky attempted to provide for syntax—"deeper" rules, in the case of use relating intents through contexts to utterances. Some of these rules will certainly be specific to discrete semantic areas (i.e. they will help to specify such things as "How we define/classify/exemplify, etc., in English.") But many (because they are "deep") will embody generalisations which will cut across notional/functional boundaries. When we have such rules we may therefore find that the arrangement of teaching materials under notional/functional headings is not the most cost-effective solution. According to such a view, present day semantic syllabuses might be seen as a temporary solution to the problem of teaching language use.[9]

Notes

1. Thanks to David Wilkins for comments on a draft of this paper. Opinions expressed are of course my own.
2. It is not, of course, only certain notional/functional approaches which prescribe "stereotypes" for language use. Many textbooks of rhetoric (for example, within the American freshman English tradition) set up models for different types of writing, which the students are expected to follow. To the extent to which this paper is polemical it is questioning the validity of such approaches as overall strategies. It is certainly my experience that most students quickly master conventions within their particular area of writing (they learn, for example, how an "English laboratory report" is usually structured). But this takes them a very short way towards being able to express their particular intents within the particular context of a piece of writing they are undertaking.
3. Johnson, 1981.
4. This diagram is *not* intended as a performance model. It merely exemplifies the aspect of communication under consideration.
5. The quotation, and indeed the link between communicative language teaching and Aristotelian rhetoric are taken from Currey (1975).
6. It will of course be argued that in some teaching situations an approach of this sort is all that is possible. It is the "phrasebook" approach, and its application can be particularly strongly argued for two types of situation—with low level students, and where there are severe time restrictions. In the former situation, the validity of a semantic approach can be questioned (see Paper 8) and one might wish to argue that at the point in the teaching operation where focusing on aspects of use becomes both feasible and desirable, such an approach provides poor fare. In the latter situation (where the validity of a semantic approach can also be questioned—cf. Paper 9) all kinds of issues concerning cost effectiveness arise. Is it better to provide a phrasebook covering a large number of semantic areas in a superficial way, or (as the second approach discussed in this paper might provide in a situation with severe time restrictions) detailed consideration of a few instances of language use?
7. Some may question the value of time spent on elaborate analysis. But this is surely particularly justified for the teaching of formal writing (whereas it may not be so for the teaching of conversational interaction) since this former involves a degree of conscious analysis. Cf. Bruner's (1975) notion of "analytic competence", mentioned in Note 1 of Paper 16.
8. The taxonomies given in the latter part of this paper are intended only to exemplify. They are based on exercise types found in Johnson (1981).
9. The proposal put forward here is the "Standpoint 4" of Paper 11. See that paper for examples of the type of "rules" which a syllabus teaching "use" might contain.

Short Annotated Bibliography

This is divided into three sections:

Section 1 Theoretical background books: basic. Highly recommended for further reading in the theoretical background to the communicative approach. Accessible to the reader without specialised knowledge in applied linguistics.

Section 2 Theoretical background books: further reading. Recommended for those seeking a more extensive knowledge. Accessible to the reader without specialised knowledge, but sometimes requiring an effort.

Section 3 Background books dealing with practical issues (especially methodology).

The lists only include books produced through recognised publishers (and which should therefore be readily available).

Section 1

1. Wilkins, D. A. *Notional Syllabuses.* Oxford University Press, 1976.

   The seminal book on the topic of notional syllabuses. There are three chapters. The first looks at the notional syllabus in relation to other syllabus types, and it is here that the distinction between "synthetic" and "analytic" is made (a distinction referred to a number of times in the present collection). For many, this chapter will be the most interesting. The second chapter gives examples of notional and functional categories (and also of a further category which Wilkins calls "modal"). The third chapter considers possible applications for the notional syllabus.

2. Widdowson, H. G. *Teaching Language as Communication.* Oxford University Press, 1978.

   Also a seminal book. The emphasis, particularly in the choice of examples, is on reading and writing rather than speaking and listening, but most of what Widdowson says is relevant to all the "four skills". The first two chapters are particularly important. Chapter 1 develops the distinction (often mentioned in this present collection) between "usage" and "use". The second chapter is a fascinating study of the nature of discourse. Later chapters look at the four skills, revealing processes which underlie them.

3. Brumfit, C. J. and Johnson, K. (eds). *The Communicative Approach to Language Teaching.* Oxford University Press, 1979.

   A collection of important papers explaining theoretical background and exploring pedagogical implications. It contains many papers referred to in the present collection. The book is divided into five parts. The first deals with linguistic, and the second with pedagogical, background. Section 3 is entitled "Applications and Techniques" and includes extracts from the Council of Europe's work. Section 4 deals with methodological perspectives. The final section is an Appendix which contains extracts from materials which might make a claim to being "communicative".

4. Trim, J. L. M., Richterich, R., van Ek, J. A. and Wilkins, D. A. *Systems Development in Adult Language Learning.* Pergamon Press, 1980.

   This collection of papers, first issued by the Council of Europe in 1973, describes the team's framework for adult language learning. All the papers deserve consideration, though some are (because of their nature) for "dipping into" rather than for reading from beginning to end. Trim's paper gives a valuable outline of the project as a whole. Richterich discusses needs analysis, and van Ek the Threshold Level. Wilkins' paper forms the basis of his later book (item 1 above).

Section 2

1. Kress, G. R. (ed). *Halliday: System and Function in Language.* Oxford University Press, 1976.

    The work of Halliday has been referred to several times in the present collection, and his view of language has certainly influenced recent approaches to language teaching. Kress presents a selection of Halliday's papers. Some are complex and will prove difficult reading; particularly useful are the first three (making up a section called "System and Function"). Other relevant papers include one on "Types of process" and another entitled "Theme and information in the English clause."

2. Coulthard, R. M. *An Introduction to Discourse Analysis.* Longman, 1977.

    Coulthard's book traces the origins of discourse analysis and discusses various areas of application. There is a short chapter on applications within language teaching, but the book's main value is as an introduction and overview of the field as a whole. Can be read by the non-specialist.

3. Sinclair, J. McH. and Coulthard, R. M. *Towards an Analysis of Discourse.* Oxford University Press, 1975.

    This book, briefly discussed in Paper 1 of the present collection, is also concerned with discourse analysis. But whereas Coulthard's book provides an overview. Sinclair and Coulthard concentrate on a restricted area of discourse—the English used by teachers and pupils in the classroom. The book's value is therefore not so much as an introduction to the field (though it does include a short review of the literature) but as a concrete example of how this type of linguistic analysis can be applied to an area of discourse. It is written in an accessible style.

4. Widdowson, H. G. *Explorations in Applied Linguistics.* Oxford University Press, 1979.

    Widdowson has played a central part in the development of communicative language teaching. This collection of his papers is less of an introduction to the field than his 1978 book (item 2 in Section 1 above), but it contains many useful and important papers. Some may prove difficult reading for the non-specialist, but in general the papers are highly approachable.

5. Byrne, D. (ed). *English Teaching Perspectives.* Longman, 1980.

    A collection of over fifty short extracts from books and articles on language teaching, accompanied by exercises and suggestions for further reading (which makes the book particularly attractive for the trainee teacher). Some of the extracts do not relate at all to the communicative approach (though they may talk good solid sense), and in many others the relevance is indirect. The reader who wishes to concentrate on the communicative approach only will therefore have to pick and choose.

6. Munby, J. *Communicative Syllabus Design.* Cambridge University Press, 1978.

    The ultimate in needs analysis models. Munby provides a sensitive and complex instrument for the analysis of language needs. The model is more complete than the Council of Europe's, and though many will find it overcomplex, the book cannot be ignored by all interested in needs analysis and ESP. The reader with only passing interest in needs analysis would do better to restrict himself to Richterich's contribution in item 4, Section 1 above.

7. van Ek, J. A. and Alexander, L. G. *Threshold Level English*. Pergamon Press, 1980.
The original version of van Ek's 1975 Council of Europe document. Useful as a reference book for anyone involved in syllabus design. Not the kind of book to read from cover to cover; but it does provide a concrete example of a semantic syllabus inventory, and can be used as a "check list" by those developing their own syllabus.
8. Stevick, E. W. *Memory, Meaning and Method*. Newbury House, 1976.
This book provides an American perspective. Although outside the European "movement" of communicative language teaching, Stevick's book is highly relevant, particularly to methodological issues. The entire book is worth reading and there are useful chapters on The Silent Way and Community Language Learning which provide the reader with an excellent opportunity to assess the extent to which such approaches are in fact "lunatic fringe".

Section 3

1. Johnson, K. and Morrow, K. E. (eds). *Communication in the Classroom*. Longman, 1981.
A collection of (specially written) papers dealing with practical issues. The book has two main parts. The first, dealing with applications for the notional syllabus, contains papers mostly written by well-known materials writers. The second is concerned with methodology. It discusses communicative techniques in relation to the "four skills", and has a section on specific techniques like drama, role play and problem solving.
2. Revell, J. *Teaching Techniques for Communicative English*. Macmillan, 1979.
A short book, intended for the classroom teacher. It does not provide an overview of the field, but contains useful suggestions for classroom techniques, particularly for the teaching of spoken English.
3. Byrne, D. *Teaching Oral English*. Longman, 1976; and *Teaching Writing Skills*. Longman, 1979.
Both these books deal with their respective topics in general terms, and without exclusive reference to a communicative approach. But both are rich in examples of communicative techniques, and each cannot be beaten as an introduction to its area. Exercises and suggestions for discussion are given throughout each book.
4. White, R. V. *Teaching Written English*. Allen & Unwin, 1980.
White's book provides less general coverage than Byrne's on the same topic, but explores the techniques of functional teaching in more depth. There are chapters dealing with specific functions like *describing objects* and *recommending*, together with a useful section on the integration of skills. Each section concludes with a clear summary stating the main points.

References

Allwright, R. L. (1977) "Language learning through communication practice." *ELT Document* **76/3**, and in Brumfit and Johnson (1979).

Austin, J. L. (1962) *How to do things with words.* Oxford University Press.

Bartlett, F. C. (1947) "The measurement of human skill." *British Medical Journal* **4510, 4511.**

Bellugi, U. (1967) "The acquisition of syntax." Unpublished doctoral dissertation, Graduate School of Education, Harvard University.

Bellugi, U. and Brown, R. (1964) *The acquisition of syntax.* University of Chicago Press.

Breen, M. P., Candlin, C. N. and Waters, A. (1979) "Communicative materials design: some basic principles." Institute of English Language Education, University of Lancaster, mimeo.

Broughton, G. (1968) *Success with English.* Penguin.

Brown, R. and Fraser, C. (1964) "The acquisition of syntax." In Bellugi and Brown (1964).

Brown, R. W. and Gilman, A. (1960) "The pronouns of power and solidarity." In Giglioli (1972).

Brumfit, C. J. (1978) " 'Communicative' language teaching: an assessment." In Strevens (1978).

Brumfit, C. J. (1979) " 'Communicative' language teaching: an educational perspective." In Brumfit and Johnson (1979).

Brumfit, C. J. and Johnson, K. (1979) *The communicative approach to language teaching.* Oxford University Press.

Bruner, J. S. (1972) *The relevance of education.* Penguin.

Bruner, J. S. (1975) "Language as an instrument of thought." In Davies (1975).

Buckler, W. E. and Sklare, A. B. (1966) *Essentials of rhetoric.* Macmillan.

Byrne, D. (1978) *Materials for language teaching: interaction packages.* Modern English Publications.

Campbell, R. and Wales, R. (1970) "The study of language acquisition." In Lyons (1970).

Candlin, C. N. (1976) "Communicative language teaching and the debt to pragmatics." Georgetown Round Table, mimeo.

Cherry, C. (1957) *On human communication.* M.I.T. Press.

Chomsky, N. (1957) *Syntactic structures.* Mouton.

Christophersen, P. (1973) *Second-language learning.* Penguin.

Condon, J. C. and Yousef, F. (1975) *An introduction to intercultural communication.* Bobbs-Merrill.

Corder, S. P. and Roulet, E. (1974) *Theoretical linguistic models in applied linguistics.* AIMAV/Didier.

Cowie, A. P. and Heaton, B. (1975) "Preparing a writing programme for students of science and technology." In Cowie and Heaton (1977).

Cowie, A. P. and Heaton, B. (1977) *English for academic purposes.* BAAL/SELMOUS.

Currey, W. B. (1975) "European syllabuses in English as a foreign language." *Language Learning* **25/2**, 1975.

Dakin, J. (1973) *The language laboratory and language learning.* Longman.

Davies, A. (1975) *Problems of language and learning.* Heinemann.

Donley, M. (1976) "The paragraph in advanced composition: a heuristic approach." *English Language Teaching Journal* **30.**

Early, P. B. (1976) "English language teaching in the Republic of Croatia, Yugoslavia: some recent developments." *ELT Documents* **76.**

Ek, J. A. van (1973) "The 'Threshold Level' in a unit/credit system." In Trim *et al.* (1980).

Ek, J. A. van (1975) "The Threshold Level." Council of Europe. Reprinted as van Ek and Alexander (1980a).

Ek, J. A. van (1978) *The Threshold Level for schools.* Longman.

Ek, J. A. van and Alexander, L. G. (1977) "Waystage." Council of Europe, Reprinted as van Ek and Alexander (1980b).

Ek, J. A. van and Alexander, L. G. (1980a) *Threshold Level English.* Pergamon Press.

Ek, J. A. van and Alexander, L. G. (1980b) *Waystage English.* Pergamon Press.

ETIC (1978) *Pre-sessional courses for overseas students.* British Council Occasional Paper.

Firth, J. R. (1957) *Papers in linguistics.* Oxford University Press.

Geddes, M. and Sturtridge, G. (1979) *Listening links.* Heinemann.

Giglioli, P. P. (1972) *Language and social context.* Penguin.

Grierson, H. J. C. (1945) *Rhetoric and English composition.* Oliver and Boyd.

Gumperz, J. J. & Hymes, D. (1970) *Directions in sociolinguistics.* Holt, Rinehart & Winston.

Halliday, M. A. K., McIntosh, A. and Strevens, P. (1964) *The linguistic sciences and language teaching.* Longman.

Halliday, M. A. K. (1970a) "The form of a functional grammar." In Kress (1976).

Halliday, M. A. K. (1970b) "Language structure and language function." In Lyons (1970).

Halliday, M. A. K. (1973) "Towards a sociological semantics." In *Explorations in the Functions of Language.* (1973) Edward Arnold. Extensive extracts in Brumfit and Johnson (1979).

Hinde, R. A. (1972) *Non-verbal communication.* Cambridge University Press.

Holden, S. (1977) *English for specific purposes.* Modern English Publications.

Hymes, D. (1970) "On communicative competence." In Gumperz and Hymes (1970). Extensive extracts in Brumfit and Johnson (1979).

Imhoof, M. and Hudson, H. (1975) *From paragraph to essay.* Longman.

Johnson, K. (1975) "Proposals concerning a new syllabus design for English language secondary school teaching in SR Croatia, Yugoslavia." British Council Archives, mimeo.

Johnson, K. (1980) " 'Systematic' and 'non-systematic' components in a communicative language teaching." Paper delivered at the Berne Colloquium in Applied Linguistics, 1980. To appear in Richterich and Widdowson (forthcoming).

Johnson, K. (1981) *Communicate in Writing.* Longman.

Johnson, K. and Morrow, K. E. (1978) *Functional materials and the classroom teacher.* Centre for Applied Language Studies, University of Reading.

Johnson, K. and Morrow, K. E. (1979) *Approaches.* Cambridge University Press.

Johnson, K. and Morrow, K. E. (1981) *Communication in the classroom.* Longman.

Jones, A. E. and Faulkner, C. (1971) *Writing good prose.* Scribner.

Jones, L. (1977) *Functions of English.* Cambridge University Press.

Kaplan, R. B. (1975) *The anatomy of rhetoric.* Harrap-Didier.

Keenan, E. L. and Ochs, E. (1979) "Becoming a competent speaker of Malagasy." In Shopen (1979).

Krashen, S. D. (1976) "Formal and informal linguistic environments in language acquisition and language learning." *TESOL Quarterly* **10**/2.

Kress, G. (1976) *Halliday: system and function in language.* Oxford University Press.

Lackstrom, J., Selinker, L. and Trimble, L. (1973) "Technical rhetorical principles and grammatical choice." *TESOL Quarterly* **7**/2.

Legge, D. (1970) *Skills.* Penguin.

Lunzer, E. A. and Morris, J. F. (1968) *Developments in human learning.* Staples.

Lyons, J. (1978) *Introduction to theoretical linguistics.* Cambridge University Press.

Lyons, J. (1970) *New horizons in linguistics.* Cambridge University Press.

Mackay, D. M. (1972) "Formal analysis of communicative process." In Hinde (1972).

Menyuk, P. (1969) *Sentences children use.* M.I.T. Press.

Morrow, K. E. (1977) *Techniques of evaluation for a notional syllabus.* Royal Society of Arts.

Morrow, K. E. and Johnson, K. (1979) *Communicate.* Cambridge University Press.

Munby, J. (1978) *Communicative syllabus design.* Cambridge University Press.

Newmark, L. (1966) "How not to interfere with language learning." *International Journal of American Linguistics* **32**/1. Reprinted in Brumfit and Johnson (1979).

Newmark, L. and Reibel, D. (1968) "Necessity and sufficiency in language learning." *International Review of Applied Linguistics* **6**/2.

O'Neill, R. (1973) *Kernel Lessons Plus.* Longman.

Pichaske, D. R. (1975) *Writing sense: a handbook of composition.* The Free Press.

Prabhu, N. S. Contribution to RIE (forthcoming).

Reed, G. F. (1968) "Skill." In Lunzer and Morris (1968).

Richterich, R. (1973) "Definition of language needs and types of adults." Reprinted in Trim *et al.* (1980).

Richterich, R. and Widdowson, H. G. (forthcoming) *The description, presentation and teaching of languages.* Hatier.

RIE (1979) "Newsletter 1 (Special Series)." Regional Institute of English South India, Bangalore.

RIE (1980) "Newsletter 4 (Special Series)." Regional Institute of English South India, Bangalore.

RIE (forthcoming) Proceedings of the seminar on "New Approaches to the Teaching of English." Held in April, 1980. Regional Institute of English South India, Bangalore.

Riley, P. (1976) "An experiment in teaching communicative competence within a restricted discourse." Paper delivered at the Neuchâtel Colloquium in Applied Linguistics, March, 1976. Mimeo.

Savignon, S. (1972) *Communicative competence: an experiment in foreign language teaching.* Center for Curriculum Development.

Searle, J. (1969) *Speech acts.* Cambridge University Press.

Shopen, T. (1979) *Languages and their speakers.* Winthrop.

Sinclair, J. and Coulthard, M. (1975) *Towards an analysis of discourse.* Oxford University Press.

Strevens, P. (1978) *In honour of A. S. Hornby.* Oxford University Press.

Trim, L. J. M. (1973) "Draft outline of a European unit/credit system for modern language learning by adults." Reprinted in Trim *et al.* (1980).

Trim, J. L. M., Richterich, R., Ek, J. A. van and Wilkins, D. A. (1980) *Systems development in adult language learning.* Pergamon Press.

Welford, A. T. (1958) "On the nature of skill." In Legge (1970).

White, R. V. (1981) Contribution to Johnson and Morrow (1981).

Widdowson, H. G. (1971) "The teaching of rhetoric to students of science and technology." Reprinted in Widdowson (1979).

Widdowson, H. G. (1972) "The teaching of English as communication." *English Language Teaching Journal* **27**/1. Reprinted in Brumfit and Johnson (1979).

Widdowson, H. G. (1973) "Two types of communication exercise." In Widdowson (1979).

Widdowson, H. G. (1978a) *Teaching language as communication.* Oxford University Press.

Widdowson, H. G. (1978b) "The acquisition and use of language systems." Paper delivered at the Berne Colloquium in Applied Linguistics, 1978, mimeo.

Widdowson, H. G. (1979) *Explorations in applied linguistics*. Oxford University Press.

Wilkins, D. A. (1973) "The linguistic and situational content of the common core in a unit/credit system." Reprinted in Trim *et al.* (1980).

Wilkins, D. A. (1974) "Notional syllabuses and the concept of a minimum adequate grammar." In Corder and Roulet (1974), and reprinted in Brumfit and Johnson (1979).

Wilkins, D. A. (1976) *Notional syllabuses*. Oxford University Press.

Woodworth, R. S. (1938) *Experimental psychology*. Holt.

Wright, A. (1976) *Visual material for the language teacher*. Longman.